Annulments and the Catholic Church

Straight Answers to Tough Questions

Edward N. Peters, J.D., J.C.D.

Foreword by
Most Reverend John J. Myers, D.D., J.C.D.,
Archbishop of Newark

ASCENSION PRESS

West Chester, Pennsylvania

Ascension Press
Post Office Box 1990
West Chester, PA 19380
Orders: 1-800-376-0520
www.AscensionPress.com

Cover design by Kinsey Caruth

Printed in the United States of America
07 08 09 10 11 12 9 8 7 6 5 4 3

ISBN 978-1-932645-00-2

CONTENTS

ACKNOWLEDGMENTS

Although the deficiencies in this book are entirely mine, its strengths draw from many sources. I am grateful to Drs. Robert Kennedy and Thomas Green of the Catholic University of America, who taught me how to read the Church's marriage law with precision and insight; to Msgr. Joseph Sadusky of the Archdiocese of Washington, who provided the best tribunal internship a student could hope to have; and to Bishop Roger Schwietz, OMI, and Fr. Dale Nau of the Diocese of Duluth, who first assigned me to tribunal duties and who patiently explained many things I should have already known. Many friends, though especially Mark Brumley, M.T.S., Fr. Joseph Koterski, S.J., and the team at Ascension Press, made suggestions that improved the revised edition of this work. Most of all, though I am grateful to Bishop Robert Brom and to the entire staff of the Tribunal of the Diocese of San Diego who, along with the appellate judges of the Province of Los Angeles, made sure that I learned something new about marriage and ministry every day.

Foreword

The sacrament of marriage is a holy institution, ordered to the good of the spouses and the procreation and education of children. In this life-giving sacramental relationship the couple establishes a partnership for life. This partnership, once validly established and consummated between the couple, is unable to be dissolved by human power. This is the great strength of marriage, that it is a partnership in which the couple is joined and spiritually nourished by God. This truth also, however, means that marriage is a serious commitment, one that should not be entered lightly. Sadly, we know that through the centuries people have entered marriage without sufficient readiness. In addition, there have always been impediments or other defects that have been understood to mar this commitment and make a marriage a non-sacramental one. Throughout the centuries the Church, in an expression of the mercy of Christ, has sought ways to investigate the possibility that a marriage might have been defective in its inception and thus not binding upon a person. Occasionally, this has allowed a person to marry again, permitting them to enter a valid sacramental union.

The legal process by which a former marriage is declared null has been described in various ways through the centuries. For the last twenty years or so, the "annulment process" has been much in vogue in the United States. Stemming from the great crisis of divorce in our society, many tribunals have seen an explosion in the amount of people seeking declarations of nullity for former marriages. Many tribunals have responded and become more efficient in a desire to extend the mercy of Christ to those in difficult situations. Almost all tribunals have staggered under the crunch. In many cases procedural and other legal norms may not have been followed as well as one might hope, and the parties involved did not always understand the nature of the process they were undertaking.

In recent years most tribunals have attempted to stabilize their practice and conform their jurisprudence more closely to the practice of the Holy See. This jurisprudence is expressed in the sentences of the Roman Rota, the highest tribunal of the Universal Church. This has led to a helpful clarification of legal norms and to a greater understanding of each tribunal's role in the search for truth in the difficult subject of marriages and annulments. Sadly for some, it has also led to confusion with the process. The annulment that they sought was not so sure and certain. The books they read and people they spoke to had assured them that they just had to fill out the papers. Yet the annulment they expected was not forthcoming.

This book will be helpful in filling a gap that has existed for some time in literature dealing with annulments. Many books have treated the legal process as merely a healing process, to assist the party to bring closure to a past marriage before embarking on another endeavor. Missing from these works was an honest explanation that not every process ends in an affirmative decision. The present book is a balanced and helpful assessment of the annulment process. It will greatly aid people in their understanding of the process and of their options for proceeding in the case of a former marriage.

The format of this work is well suited to deal with the specific questions which often surface in the annulment process. The book is organized into various sections and this should assist those who are confused by a particular aspect of the process. Included is general information about annulments and about the various officials involved. The information provided on the possible grounds for an annulment should help clarify some often-asked questions. Often, people seeking annulments have complicated questions. Some typical ones are included by Dr. Peters, and these questions will help the reader identify their own situation in the examples given.

A few sections in particular should be highlighted as being highly valuable. Many works on annulments ignore the possibility that the process could end in a negative response. Dr. Peters includes insightful information for those who do receive a negative decision. Inclusion of this material acknowledges the reality of the canonical process, prepares the reader for that possible outcome, and may assist those who are frustrated or dismayed after having received a negative sentence. Another valuable section includes questions for those who are not seeking an annulment but who are nonetheless involved in the process. These include former spouses and parties who are called upon to be witnesses. Helpful information is provided for these parties, who may be confused as to why they are being requested to provide information.

The annulment process combines the difficult task of upholding Our Lord's strong teaching on marriage, yet extending his mercy to those whose former marriages might have been sacramentally null. *Annulments and the Catholic Church: Straight Answers to Tough Questions* should prove to be a highly valuable resource for those interested in this delicate area.

—Most Reverend John J. Myers, D.D., J.C.D.,
Archbishop of Newark

INTRODUCTION

Each year more than a hundred thousand people, including thousands of non-Catholics, are directly involved in the Church's annulment process. Several times that number—family members and friends—are affected by the decisions reached in annulment cases. All of these people, to say nothing of observers from the Catholic and the non-Catholic world, have questions about annulments. Most of the questions contained in these pages derive from those posed to me as a canon lawyer, tribunal official, and teacher over the years. Indeed, I have found that people's questions touch on almost every significant aspect of the annulment process, and so it was not difficult to cover most of the key issues in a question-and-answer format. I have tried to answer these questions as I would address someone sitting in my office—that is, simply and accurately. There are, though, two advantages to answering annulment questions in writing: First, I can add a few extra details to written answers, usually concerning things that people are likely to pose as follow-ups to their original question; second, I can give references to the canon numbers upon which my answers are based. Obviously, I think the answers in this book are correct, but if one wishes to disagree with them, at least it will be clear why I said what I said. Speaking of being clear, I have avoided technical terms as much as possible in these pages, but this is a technical field and precision comes with technical terminology. Major terms are defined in the Glossary.

This book can be read front-to-back, since the questions generally proceed in the same order in which they arise during a typical annulment case. The Index, on the other hand, allows for consultation on a topical basis, since there is no need to explain earlier issues if only the later ones are causing confusion.

A word of caution: Do not take this book and try to analyze your own marriage, or your parents' marriage, or your children's marriages, or your friends' marriages (see Question 100). Do not take it to a pastor or tribunal judge and say, "See? It says right here this annulment must be granted (or denied)." Because this book does not say that.

Every annulment case is heard under the same set of laws, but no two annulment cases present anything like the same set of facts. The information in this book is provided in the context of a specific question, but even these questions exist in a larger and more complex context. This is why judging is both a science and an art.

In any event, it should be obvious that this book is designed neither to encourage more annulment cases nor to discourage them. Actually, this book couldn't do either, since the canon law under which annulment cases are adjudicated is already in force, and the facts assessed in an annulment case are already in place before a canon lawyer ever sees them. To put it another way, the information in this book can be used legitimately by some people to advance annulment petitions they desire and by others to resist annulment petitions they oppose. My hope in both situations is to help the people involved in or affected by the annulment process to understand the process better and to participate in it more effectively. If this, in turn, helps to ensure that the decisions reached by diocesan tribunals in annulment cases are as accurate as possible, I shall be satisfied.

—Dr. Edward Neal Peters

NOTES

- "1983 CIC" means "1983 Code of Canon Law" (*Codex Iuris Canonici*), promulgated by Pope John Paul II in 1983 and currently in force. The number(s) immediately following "1983 CIC" refer to the actual canons of the 1983 Code. All canonical references in this work are to the 1983 Code of Canon Law unless expressly stated otherwise.

- "1917 CIC" means "1917 Code of Canon Law" (*Codex Iuris Canonici*), promulgated by Pope Benedict XV in 1917 and no longer in force. The number(s) immediately following "1917 CIC" refer to the actual canons of the 1917 Code.

- Unless otherwise noted, diocesan and archdiocesan institutions follow the same rules in marriage nullity cases.

- For purposes of readability, some questions and answers are phrased as if coming from a husband or a wife, but in no case does the answer depend on the gender of the questioner.

- All opinions expressed in this work are the author's. If any opinions expressed herein are inconsistent with the mind of the Church, then the Church's judgment prevails.

CHAPTER 1

BASIC QUESTIONS ON ANNULMENTS

Question 1: **What is an annulment?**

Considering that American tribunals declare well over fifty-thousand annulments each year (with eighty-thousand being declared annually worldwide), the answer to your question might come as a surprise: The term annulment is nowhere used or defined in the Catholic Church's Code of Canon Law. Imprecisions of popular language notwithstanding, the reality of an annulment is fairly easy to explain. An annulment (more accurately termed a declaration of matrimonial nullity) is an official determination by an ecclesiastical tribunal that what appeared to be a valid marriage was actually not one. An annulment is not a finding that the spouses never really loved each other, nor that the divorce was more one party's fault than the other's, nor that one party is a better Catholic than the other. It is merely a juridic determination that, at the time of the wedding, one or both parties to the marriage lacked sufficient capacity for marriage, or that one or both parties failed to give adequately their consent to marriage as the Church understands and proclaims it, or in weddings involving at least one Catholic, that the parties violated the Church's requirements of canonical form in getting married.

In finding a marriage null, the Church does not cast blame on either or both parties, even if one or both of them acted in a blameworthy manner. Instead, the Church only states that it does not consider itself or its members bound to accept the consequences of the wedding ceremony in question. In practical terms, after nullity is declared (if it is declared), the Church considers the parties free of the marriage bond that would have otherwise arisen (1983 CIC 1134). The parties are, therefore, generally free to contract marriage in the Church.

Question 2: How is an annulment different from a divorce?

I know, of course, that many people refer to annulments as "Catholic divorces," but divorces and annulments differ in fundamental ways. Still, it might be good to begin by seeing what they have in common. A divorce and an annulment are similar in that they both are legal declarations that are necessary before one person can marry another, if either of them has been married before and the former spouse is not deceased. But this is about where the similarities end and the important differences begin.

A divorce is a civil judicial act whereby what was a civilly valid marriage is officially broken, terminated, ended, finished, *kaput*—whatever word you want to use. The point is, the state makes no secret about its claimed power to separate what it once joined. (I hedge a bit on conceding the state power to separate what it joined because, in many cases, what it joined is a valid marriage under natural law, and hence it is something the state is not free to tinker with. But that is a different problem.)

An annulment, on the other hand, is an ecclesiastical judicial determination whereby what was believed to be a valid marriage is declared never to have been a marriage in the first place. An annulment does not deny that a relationship, perhaps a long and serious one, existed between the parties. It does not imply that the parties were "living in sin" or that the children are illegitimate. It only states that, as a matter of objective canon law, what was believed to be a valid marriage in the eyes of the Church was not so.

There is, by the way, something called a *civil annulment*, and this is based on some of the same concepts as ecclesiastical annulments. For example, if someone who is civilly married attempts to marry another person, we call that bigamy. If the second spouse finds out about the prior marriage, he or she probably cannot sue for a civil divorce; instead, a civil *annulment* of the marriage is in order based on the prior marriage of the other party. In such cases, the state generally considers the second spouse not to be divorced but rather never to have been married at all. Civil annulments, in the relatively rare cases in which they are granted, are not the equivalent of ecclesiastical annulments, even though the concept is similar. Marriages that end in civil annulment must still be adjudicated ecclesiastically before canonical nullity can be declared.

Question 3: **One more time. What's the difference between a divorce and an annulment? They still seem mighty similar to me.**

Well, as an analogy, consider automobiles and ambulances. They are both four-wheeled, gasoline-powered vehicles that drive on roads and take people places. They would seem to be rather similar in many respects. Now, let me ask you: This afternoon, would you rather leave work in a car or in an ambulance? What seems similar in some respects can be as different as night and day in others. Divorce destroys something that was; annulments recognize that something never was. That is not just semantics, any more than describing one's trip home from the office as being in a car rather than in an ambulance is just semantics. It is a matter of precision and hence a matter of truth. Last night my boys played catch with an apple, but neither of them tried to eat a baseball for supper. There are similarities between divorce and annulment, of course, although these similarities are routinely exaggerated, and even exploited, by the secular media and others. Thoughtful people, however, will avoid treating things like divorce and annulment, though similar in some respects, as if they were necessarily similar in others.

Question 4: Who should I see first about getting an annulment?

Virtually every nullity petition begins at the parish level with an interview in the pastor's office. This is a practically useful but technically unofficial part of most diocesan tribunals' procedures. Most pastors (or their staffs) are very willing to assist potential petitioners in drafting their forms for the tribunal. You should realize, though, that contacting the pastor, or even dropping off your completed nullity petition with him or the parish staff, is not the official beginning of your case. Only when the tribunal itself receives and formally accepts your petition do any procedural clocks start ticking. If several weeks pass after talking with your pastor and you still have not heard anything from the tribunal, check into it. Paperwork can be misplaced or misfiled, or there might be some other problem affecting your petition. If you have reasons for not wishing to approach your local parish first, you can call or write directly to your diocesan office for guidance. (It is listed in the phone book.) Ask for the tribunal.

Question 5: **I understand that I need an annulment, but I do not understand why I have to pay for it. It is a Church rule that I have to have an annulment. Why should I have to pay for its rules?**

The state required you to get a civil divorce before it would allow you to remarry under its laws, right? The state also required you to pay certain fees and court costs, right? Do you think it was unfair of the state to make you pay for one of its rules? Technically, of course, you were not paying for a civil divorce (as if you could literally buy one); instead you were paying for the juridic process by which that divorce was officially effected. Similarly, one does not pay for an annulment (as if it were for sale); rather one pays for the juridic process by which an annulment might be declared. Notice I say *might* be declared. Unlike a civil divorce, an annulment is not a more or less automatic process in which one has an eventual right to a certain outcome. Because of the Church's commitment to marriage, the annulment process is concerned with very different and usually much more complex types of issues than is a civil divorce court. The ecclesiastical process requires the attention of highly trained officials and a qualified supporting staff. The documentation and record-keeping required is considerable. Now, just as a civil court derives its support from a combination of general taxes and specific user fees, so a diocesan tribunal is supported by the general contributions of the faithful and additional fees paid by those using its special services. No one should think, by the way, that diocesan tribunals, American or otherwise, are making money on the annulment process, and indeed, no diocesan tribunal I know of operates in the black. American tribunals generally charge users about one-half of the actual cost of a marriage case, and in almost all cases, the out-ofpocket expenses incurred in an ecclesiastical annulment fall far below those incurred in a civil divorce.of course, when an individual truly cannot meet his or her share of the costs, procedures for reducing or waiving tribunal fees are available (1983 CIC 1464, 1649). No one is ever denied his or her "day in the tribunal" because of an inability to pay.

Question 6: How much does an annulment cost?

Costs vary, but typically they will parallel the general cost of living in the United States, tending therefore to be more expensive on the East and West Coasts and in urban areas but less expensive in the Midwest and South. Annulment costs fall into three main types. First and most commonly, there are the basic petition fees payable to the tribunal. This is what most people refer to when they talk about the cost of an annulment. In the U.S. most tribunals charge anywhere from $200 to $1,000 for adjudicating a standard nullity case. A few tribunals charge over $1,000, and a few charge nothing at all, but *all* tribunals state in advance what the total fee is for processing a petition (1983 CIC 1649). The fee for "documentary cases" (that is, cases eligible for the expedited process provided for by canon 1686) is usually much less, $25 or so being common. If multiple petitions are presented by the same petitioner simultaneously, he or she should expect to pay all or most of the standard fee for each case, especially if they are the less expensive documentary cases.

Although there is, strictly speaking, authority on the part of the tribunal to assess fees on both parties in a marriage case (1983 CIC 1649), this is almost never done. Rather, the petitioner—that is, the person who files for the annulment—almost always pay all fees associated with a marriage nullity case. These fees are typically payable over time, and there are means for having fees reduced or eliminated in cases of financial hardship (1983 CIC 1464).

In addition to basic tribunal fees, there are sometimes additional costs incurred in consulting with medical, psychological, or other experts for resolution of a nullity case (see 1983 CIC 1580, 1649). These fees are usually the responsibility of the petitioner. Again, if you are unsure what fees are required, ask the tribunal.

Finally, some additional costs could be incurred if one were to require, say, certain witnesses to travel a long distance or to produce unusual kinds of evidence (1983 CIC 1571). Or, one might wish to engage a canonical advocate of one's own choosing rather than accepting an advocate supplied by the tribunal. In such cases it is likely that the individual requiring such services will be required to pay for them (but see canon 1490, that encourages diocesan tribunals to keep canon lawyers on staff to assist parties in marriage nullity cases). Questions about these potential additional expenses should be presented at the beginning of the case, or in any event as soon as they arise.

What is important to take from all of this is that the stories about $20,000 annulments are myth. Conceivably, if a person files in the most expensive diocesan tribunal, uses extensive medical and psychological testimony, and appeals the case through various levels of ecclesiastical courts, he or she could incur a bill of some thousands of dollars. But such cases are very rare, and most annulments are processed from beginning to end for a fraction of that.

Question 7: How long will my annulment take?

Church law requires that tribunals handle all cases as quickly as possible and usually in the order they are received (1983 CIC 1458). From the time your completed application is presented to the tribunal (with all required documents and sufficient witness responses), you should expect a decision in about twelve months (1983 CIC 1453). Cases that present clear canonical grounds for nullity and that are supported by canonically strong evidence can be processed even more quickly (1983 CIC 1606). It is important to realize that what counts is the *tribunal's* assessment of these factors, not your assessment of them.

It is possible to have a nullity case taken out of turn for good reason (1983 CIC 1458), but the tribunal's judgment here is the controlling factor. The "I've-already-booked-a-reception-hall" argument is not usually considered a good reason for a tribunal to take a marriage case out of turn. Reasons that are sometimes accepted as justifying speedier treatment (though not necessarily the desired results) would include the intended entry of a party into the Church at Easter. But parties—and pastors—should not expect tribunals to drop everything else at the mere sight of an "RCIA case."

The mandatory review that is part of every case in which an annulment is declared can take up to six additional months, but it usually requires less than that. And for marriage nullity cases that are filed in Rome or that go there on appeal (1983 CIC 1444), there really is no practical time limit. Two to four years is not unusual.

Generally speaking, one should not call the tribunal office just to ask about the "status" of one's case. Phone calls only interrupt the tribunal staff's heavy workload, and they cannot speed up your case. Instead, drop the office a letter or postcard if you are concerned about the time your case is requiring.

Question 8: **Are annulments easier to get nowadays than they used to be?**

Yes, without a doubt, for two very important reasons:

First, numerous reforms in the canons that govern matrimonial nullity cases have greatly facilitated the ability of Catholics and non-Catholics to file and pursue marriage nullity petitions in diocesan tribunals. These revisions, placed in Church law by the Holy See (not by creative American canonists), have been in force more or less since the early 1970s and for the most part were made standard in the 1983 Code. They include a host of revisions on technical points, that while perhaps escaping the immediate notice of non-canonists, carried an immediate impact on both the number of nullity petitions filed and the percentage of petitions granted.

Second, reforms in the canons that govern important matters related to matrimonial consent have been revised by Rome. It is now much easier to examine directly the matrimonial impact of many negative and seriously-debilitating factors like drug and alcohol abuse, physical and sexual abuse, parental divorce and serial marriage, and other psychological and emotional factors. Any of these factors can seriously impact a marriage before it ever gets off the ground, sometimes to the point of canonical nullity. The Congregation for the Doctrine of the Faith (that few could accuse of being lax on marriage) has recognized in its letter *On the Reception of Communion by Divorced and Remarried Catholics* (September 14, 1994; paragraph 9) the effects of canonical revisions in increasing the chances of proving the canonical nullity of a marriage. In brief, the bases for matrimonial nullity in real life are now easier to prove in canon law.

Understandably, the speed and force with which these revisions have impacted Catholic nullity cases (particularly during times when so much deterioration in other aspects of Catholic life seems to have set in) have caused many to conclude that the tribunal process is partly responsible for the ongoing collapse of Catholic (and secular) marriage. These criticisms can and should be rejected, without going to the opposite extreme of claiming that diocesan tribunals are flawless in their handling of nullity cases. They are not; they cannot be.

If an analogy may be used here, the revised canons on matrimonial capacity and consent might not serve as a cure for the divorce disease, but they do greatly aid in the diagnosis of the condition. Church teaching on the permanence of marriage has not changed and never will change because it is the teaching of Jesus Himself (see Mt 19:3-9). But the Church's ability to determine more precisely just what a null marriage looks like *has* improved. Admittedly, it might not be a pretty sight, but it is a more accurate picture than before.

If correctly followed, the annulment process can declare certain people free to marry in the Church who should be so recognized. It also frequently shows them how their earlier attempt(s) at marriage were invalid, making them, one would hope, much less likely to repeat the same mistakes. For those denied an annulment, the process of seeking one can affirm that, notwithstanding their civil divorce and the suffering that both preceded and followed it, the Church still considers them married and expects them to conduct themselves in accord with that status to the extent that they are able.

Question 9: Will the length of time two people were married make any difference in an annulment case?

Yes and no. Strictly speaking, the duration of a marriage is not proof of either its validity or invalidity, though it could be used as evidence of either. Remember, an annulment case focuses on what happened prior to and at the time of the wedding. Any post-wedding evidence, such as the length of the marriage, is useful only to the degree that it helps illuminate the parties' statuses and actions in actually getting married.

For example, a couple who remain together for a long period of time pretty obviously have some relational skills and some capacity for life together. That evidence tends to point toward the validity of their marriage. At the same time, canon law recognizes a principle from the Middle Ages: "What was infirm at the beginning cannot be made firm just by the passage of time." There are marriages that lasted many decades yet were later proven to be null.

On the other hand, a couple who remain together for just a few days or weeks give some evidence that they really had no idea what marriage was all about in the first place. Therefore one can argue that they never entered what the Church would recognize as a valid marriage. However, the mere brevity of the marriage (that is, the couple's failure to live in accord with the permanence of marriage) does not necessarily mean that they were incapable of entering a true marriage. Just as above, there are marriages that "lasted" only a few months but that could not be proven canonically null.

Question 10: Is it true that one cannot receive an annulment if the marriage produced children?

No, it is not. The presence of children is not proof or even evidence that a marriage was valid, and the absence of children is not proof or evidence that it was invalid.

CHAPTER 2

OFFICIALS IN THE PROCESS

Question 11: **Do I have any choice over the judge(s) who will hear my marriage case?**

Not really. Judges are appointed to office by the diocesan bishop (1983 CIC 1421), and they are assigned to specific cases by the judicial vicar (1983 CIC 1425 § 3), usually in the order the cases are presented (1983 CIC 1458). That said, if you have reason to object to a certain judge's participation in your case, you have the right to make that objection known under canon 1448. The same thing applies to objections against Promoters of Justice and Defenders of the Bond, auditors (1983 CIC 1428 § 1), and assessors (1983 CIC 1424) involved in your case. Your objection need not be accepted by the tribunal, although in my experience most tribunals try to accommodate reasonable objections from either petitioners or respondents.

Question 12: **I was quite surprised when I showed up for an interview on my annulment case. I was interviewed by a nun who called herself a judge. I thought canon lawyers were priests. Is this going to cause a problem in my case?**

From time to time I have seen the same look of surprise in someone's eyes when he or she arrives for a tribunal interview with me, a married layman.

The great majority of canon lawyers are priests, but deacons, religious, and laity make up a growing percentage of the profession. Canon law requires all tribunal judges to be degreed in canon law (1983 CIC 1421 § 3), but it allows bishops to appoint academically qualified lay judges in diocesan tribunals (1983 CIC 1421 § 2). When lay persons, like myself, serve as judges in tribunals, they do so together with two clerics (usually priests) serving as collegiate judges.

It can happen, moreover, that one of the three judges, perhaps the lay judge, is more active in the instruction of a particular case than are the other two. For example, the judicial vicar (or his adjutant) might have assigned the lay judge to serve as *ponens,* or primary author, of the decision for the case (1983 CIC 1429, 1610 § 2). Even though all judges in a collegiate tribunal must pass on the entire acts of a case and decide each case by majority vote (1983 CIC 1426 § 1), one would expect to see the *ponens* more directly involved in the actual development of a case that he or she has to write up.

Question 13: Can bishops grant annulments?

Strictly speaking, yes, but this would be very rare. Canon 1419 § 1 recognizes the diocesan bishop (but not auxiliary, coadjutor, or retired bishops) as the first judge in a diocese, and canon 1425 § 4 could be invoked to allow the diocesan bishop to sit as the sole judge of a marriage case. But all American diocesan bishops have appointed judicial vicars and other judges in their dioceses (1983 CIC 1420, 1421) and, to my knowledge, no bishop has ever exercised his option to reserve the hearing of marriage nullity cases to himself. If he were to do so, however, he would still be required to follow the canons governing the adjudication of marriage nullity cases.

Question 14: **Can pastors grant annulments?**

Insofar as they are acting in their capacity as pastors, certainly not. Pastors, as pastors, have no judicial authority under the 1983 Code. But be careful here: Under the 1917 Code, which was less strict about judges needing canon law degrees than is the 1983 Code, many pastors also served as tribunal judges, at least for certain types of "simpler" cases (for example, lack of form cases). Some of these synodal and prosynodal judges, as they were technically known (1917 CIC 1574), served in judicial office until 1993 or so. Conceivably, a few are even yet in judicial office, although in all the cases I have seen, Vatican officials have refused to allow such non-degreed judges to renew their terms of service.

Additional confusion on this point can arise because many pastors are currently delegated by their bishops to grant certain types of dispensations. (A dispensation is a special ecclesiastical authorization that allows a marriage to take place despite canons that would otherwise prevent such a marriage from being recognized in the Church. A common example would be a dispensation that allows a Catholic to marry a non-baptized person, even though canon 1086 generally outlaws such marriages.) In general, if a pastor, or any other priest, claims the authority to annul any type of marriage without going through the diocesan tribunal, check it out.

Question 15: **I have been told that the Defender of the Bond is opposed to my annulment. Who is this Defender of the Bond and what has this got to do with my case?**

In 1741 Pope Benedict XIV enacted a major series of canonical reforms, including reforms on the conduct of matrimonial cases in diocesan tribunals. Ever since then, the Defender of the Bond is a tribunal official in every diocese whose task it is to propose, without regard to the opinions of the parties, everything that can be reasonably argued against granting a nullity petition. The role of the Defender, as Pope Pius XII said in 1944, and as Pope John Paul II reaffirmed in the 1983 Code (see 1983 CIC 1432), is not to stall marriage nullity cases with a myriad of technicalities but rather to make sure that all of the evidence in favor of the marriage is carefully considered by the judges.

The Defender of the Bond is appointed by the diocesan bishop, and he or she can be either a cleric or a lay person who is academically degreed in canon law (1983 CIC 1435). The Defender does not work for the respondent nor, strictly speaking, against the petitioner. The Defender literally defends the bond that Church law presumes to have arisen from a presumptively valid marriage (1983 CIC 1134).

In many of the cases coming before diocesan tribunals, there are, unfortunately, few reasonable arguments against granting a nullity petition. To such cases the Defender cannot raise substantive objections, although he or she still monitors them to make sure that procedural requirements are honored.

But when a Defender does raise substantive (or procedural, for that matter) objections to declaring nullity in a case, the judges must seriously consider these objections. Defenders are usually as well trained in canon law as judges are. Some Defenders have prior experience as judges, and many judges once served as Defenders. In brief, Defenders and judges usually understand what the other is saying.

If a Defender of the Bond does not like the result in a case, he or she can appeal it to a higher court, even over the objections of both parties to the marriage (1983 CIC 1628). This alone makes Defenders a force to be reckoned with. Even so, Defenders do not have veto power over judges' decisions, and their objections to the granting of an annulment can be overruled.

Do not think of the Defender of the Bond as an obstacle to your nullity petition. Think of him or her as a sign of the Church's commitment to canonical quality control in general and to the protection of marriage in particular. If the Defender has objections to your petition, they will be taken seriously. But you still have the right to disagree with the Defender (see, for example, 1983 CIC 1601, 1603) if you feel that the tribunal erred in siding with the Defender, you have the same right to appeal the tribunal's decision as the Defender has to appeal the opposite result.

Question 16: Who is the Promoter of Justice?

The Promoter of Justice is an official the bishop appoints to look after the public good (1983 CIC 1430, 1435). Like Defenders of the Bond, the Promoter can be either a cleric or a lay person, as long as he or she is degreed in canon law (1983 CIC 1435). Nullity cases do not usually require the participation of a Promoter, but Promoters are allowed to intervene in marriage nullity cases if they feel the public good is at risk (1983 CIC 1430, 1691). The only time one might see a Promoter becoming involved in a nullity case would be if canon 1674 were being invoked to allow the Promoter to impugn a certain marriage.

Question 17: May the parties in an annulment case use lawyers?

If by lawyer you mean a civil lawyer (perhaps the one who handled your divorce), the answer is no. Canon 1481 allows the parties in marriage nullity cases to use canon lawyers, known as advocates, but to qualify as a canonical advocate, one must meet the requirements listed in canon 1483: (1) be at least eighteen years old; (2) enjoy a good reputation; (3) be an expert in canon law; and (4) be approved by the diocesan bishop. Very few civil lawyers (even divorce lawyers or Catholic lawyers) know much about canon law, and they would therefore not be qualified to serve as canonical advocates. There is no requirement that either or both parties in a marriage case use canonical advocates, and many nullity cases are conducted without them. This stems from the fact that canon law tends to preserve the Roman inquiry-based approach, in which advocates assist tribunals in the discovery of truth. (This approach contrasts with the American common law, or adversarial, system in which lawyers and their clients "win" or "lose.") Theoretically, at least, no one loses in a marriage case, although that truth might at times require an exceptionally open mind for appreciation. When advocates are used, however, they assume certain rights and responsibilities in the process, that are explained to the parties at the time.

To the surprise of some, there is no requirement that advocates be academically degreed in canon law. Personally, I think the day is coming when all advocates will have to be degreed in canon law. The current law recognizes that some people have developed very impressive canonical knowledge and skills, at least in marriage nullity cases, as a result of long experience in the field.

Many American dioceses use parish priests and deacons as advocates in marriage nullity cases. Typically, the priest or deacon who helps the petitioner apply for the annulment also serves as advocate for that party, and advocates for respondents are often appointed from among tribunal staff. Some parishes even have lay or religious "annulment coordinators" who assist the parties in their cases. A few dioceses are moving toward certification of non-degreed parish advocates, whether laity or clergy, to help with the huge marriage caseload currently being addressed by diocesan tribunals.

Nevertheless, and despite my respect for the work of many non-degreed advocates, the parties to a marriage case have certain rights in the selection of the canonical counsel, including the right to qualified counsel. Canon law judges are allowed to be more flexible in assisting parties to formulate their canonical cases than civil judges are allowed to be (1983 CIC 1452 § 2), but I have still seen cases whose outcomes could have been influenced by the quality of the advocates working on them.

Question 18: **Can I pick my own canon lawyer?**

Yes, generally speaking, but there are a few strings attached. Canon 1481 establishes the right of the parties in all tribunal cases to pick their own canon lawyers, but that same canon also allows parties to act without a canon lawyer under most circumstances, if they so choose. The canon states that automatic canonical counsel need not be appointed by the diocesan tribunal in marriage nullity cases. On the other hand, diocesan tribunals are encouraged (but not required) to have canon lawyers attached to and paid by the tribunal, being thereby available to assist parties wishing to use them in marriage nullity cases (1983 CIC 1490). Most American tribunals will probably say that they meet this exhortation, but often they do this by means of making available persons who are judges in other marriage nullity cases. These serve as advocates in cases in which they will not be called upon to render a decision. While such a system is probably not what the Code had in mind, it is, in most cases, a practical way of satisfying the legitimate and rising demand for canonical advocacy services without incurring the large overhead of retaining designated advocates. In any event, even if the diocesan tribunal hearing your marriage case has advocates available, you retain the right to name your own canon lawyer, provided that he or she meets the standards set forth in canon 1483 (namely, being over eighteen, possessing a decent reputation, being expert—though not necessarily degreed—in canon law, and being approved by the local bishop). This last clause—being approved by the local bishop—is meant to be taken seriously, of course, but so is one's basic right to name one's own canonical advocate.

The trend seems to be toward allowing parties as much freedom as possible in naming their own advocates. This is not only because such a policy is more consistent with canon law but also because those usually requested to serve as personal advocates are almost always academically degreed and well-trained, and because the fees incurred thereby are usually the responsibility of the party choosing them. Conceivably, however, a party wishing to name an advocate (especially one from outside the diocese) might be told that a given tribunal does not accept outside advocates. In my opinion, such an answer is canonically illegal, and there are means available to you and your intended advocate to contest that decision.

A few additional points: One can name several advocates to serve simultaneously (1983 CIC 1482 § 3), although this would rarely be needed, and written appointments of advocates (known as *mandates*) must be presented to the tribunal at the beginning of representation (1983 CIC 1484 § 1). Once appointed, advocates assume certain rights and duties (see canons 1482, 1489), that are explained at the time of appointment. It is useful to know that one can remove one's advocate at any time by giving notice to the advocate and to the judge (1983 CIC 1486 § 1). Moreover, for serious cause, an advocate can be removed from office by the judge (1983 CIC 1487).

Question 19: **What role would the priest who married us play in our annulment case?**

He need not play any role. There is no canonical requirement that the official witness to a wedding be made part of an annulment case based on that wedding (1983 CIC 1108, 1112). On the other hand, either or both parties could ask that the officiating minister be called as a witness in the case. Normally, one would only do that if the minister had significant knowledge of either or both parties independently of the ceremony. If, however, some serious situation affecting the ceremony itself was in question, it would make sense to bring in the minister to testify about it.

CHAPTER 3

WHERE CAN ANNULMENT CASES BE HEARD?

Question 20: Where can my annulment petition be heard?

Virtually all marriage nullity cases are heard in diocesan tribunals, the offices of which are usually located in or very near diocesan administrative centers (which are listed in the phone book). What you are probably asking is which tribunal or tribunals would be competent (that is, canonically qualified) to hear your case. The rules on tribunal competence—that is, the authority of a given diocesan tribunal to adjudicate a marriage case—are generous, but they must be followed carefully lest the results of a case be overturned (1983 CIC 1620). The tribunal will, of course, handle issues related to competence, but an explanation of what it is doing might be helpful.

Canon 1673 determines which diocesan tribunals can hear a case. It is divided into four parts, any one of which is sufficient to establish canonical competence to hear a case:

1) *Place of the wedding.* The tribunal of the diocese where the wedding was celebrated, known canonically as "the forum of contract," is always competent to hear a nullity petition on that marriage. This rule applies even if one or both spouses have since left that diocese, and even if they were only there long enough for the wedding to

take place and never had any intention of remaining there. It also applies regardless of the possible objection of the *respondent*— that is, the spouse other than the one who filed the nullity petition. The respondent's opinion on this point need not even be solicited. And it applies to cases of non-Catholic weddings, even if neither party has since become Catholic. (Note: If the wedding to be impugned was a Catholic wedding, but one that had been preceded by a civil wedding, it is the place of the Catholic wedding and not the civil ceremony that is considered the forum of contract.)

2) *Place of the respondent.* The tribunal of the diocese where the respondent has canonical domicile or quasi-domicile (basically, one's place of residence, 1983 CIC 102-107) known canonically as "the forum of the respondent," is always competent to hear a nullity petition on that marriage. There are a few technical variations on this rule, such as in cases dealing with transient or mentally-incompetent respondents. This rule basically means that any diocese in which the respondent is living and has lived for at least three months (sometimes less) is competent to hear a petition on that respondent's marriage (see 1983 CIC 100, 107). This rule applies even if the petitioner has never been in the respondent's forum and even if neither party is Catholic.

As is true for forum of contract, the rules on forum of the respondent apply regardless of the possible objection of the respondent, whose opinion on this point need not even be solicited. Moreover, even if the respondent leaves the territory after the tribunal has obtained jurisdiction over the case (1983 CIC 1512, n.2), the petition can still be heard.

3) *Place of the petitioner.* Under certain circumstances, the petitioner can submit his or her marriage case to the

tribunal where he or she currently lives, regardless of where the wedding took place or where the respondent currently lives. This is often more convenient for the petitioner, and tens of thousands of marriage nullity cases are heard this way each year. But the rules are a little trickier.

First, the petitioner must canonically have a domicile, not just a quasi-domicile, in the diocese in which he or she wishes to file the nullity petition. This means that the petitioner must have, at some point, moved into the diocese with the intention of remaining there unless called away (1983 CIC 102). Note that domicile for the petitioner (or respondent, for that matter) can be acquired immediately. This might sound a little strange at first, and it could strike some as a vague rule, but in practice it is fairly easy to assess accurately. Moreover, regardless of one's intention about staying in a diocese, mere residence in the diocese for five years automatically confers domicile.

Second, both parties must live in the territory of the same conference of bishops. In most cases this simply means that both parties must live in the same country, since most episcopal conferences cover one and only one nation (1983 CIC 448 § 1). In the United States, though, there are some American territories that do not belong to the National Conference of Catholic Bishops: For example, Puerto Rico, Guam, and other U.S. possessions in the South Pacific are not considered part of the U.S. for purposes of matrimonial jurisdiction under canon 1673, n. 3. On the other hand, the Virgin Islands are part of the U.S. for purposes of this canon.

Third, it is up to the judicial vicar of the diocese where the respondent has domicile to consent to the request for competence from the petitioner's diocese. Without that consent, the case cannot be heard in the petitioner's home diocese. Before granting such consent, moreover, the judicial vicar of the respondent must get the opinion of the respondent on the request. Note that it is not required that the respondent *agree* to the request for competence, only that his or her judicial vicar has gotten the views of the respondent (even a non-Catholic respondent) on the matter.

Most requests for competence made under canon 1673, n. 3, are granted, probably because most respondents do not in fact oppose a "foreign" tribunal's hearing their case. The few respondents who do express objections usually object to *any* tribunal's hearing the case, something that respondents clearly have no right to inhibit.

On the other hand, a respondent who expresses objections based on serious inconvenience in participation has a better chance of getting his or her judicial vicar to withhold the desired consent. It is not necessary for respondents to use technical words in expressing their objections, as long as they are clear enough in their objections to give their judicial vicar a reason to say no. Of course, if the respondent's judicial vicar does say no, there is nothing to prevent the petitioner from then filing his or her case in the respondent's diocesan tribunal or in the place of contract.

4) *Place of proofs.* Under certain circumstances a petitioner can seek to have his or her petition filed in any convenient tribunal, provided that the desired tribunal can be shown to be what canon law considers the *forum of proofs* under canon 1673, n. 4. In some respects this is similar to the request for the *forum of petitioner* discussed above.

In these cases the petitioner approaches a diocesan tribunal (not necessarily one in which the petitioner has domicile or quasi-domicile) and asks it to consider accepting the case under canon 1673, n. 4. The petitioner provides evidence that the tribunal really is the forum in which the evidence in the case could be best collected. This might be the case, for example, if several of the witnesses who know the details of the marriage are located in or near that diocese or if important documents are more easily produced there than in other places. The diocesan tribunal would still have to obtain the consent of the judicial vicar of the diocese where the ex-spouse has domicile, but unlike the situation under canon 1673, n. 3, there is no requirement under canon 1673, n. 4, that the respondent live in the territory of the same episcopal conference as the petitioner. That difference makes canon 1673, n. 4 a basis for jurisdiction in some of the more unusual cases such as those involving parties from different countries.

Finally, one should note that there is no preference among the four bases for jurisdiction listed above, and they can be pursued at the petitioner's choice (1983 CIC 1407 § 3, 1415). In other words, there is no requirement that petitioners file in the forum of contract before filing in the forum of respondent and so on.

***Question 21:* My former wife and I were married in a Third World country. After our divorce, I came to America and I was planning to seek an annulment. However, I have been told that I will have to have my case heard in that country because my ex-wife still lives there. Is this true?**

Not necessarily. There are two possible ways to have your case heard in the United States (or any other nation, for that matter).

First, you can present your petition to any convenient U.S. tribunal and ask it to consider accepting the case under canon 1673, n. 4, the *forum of proofs* discussed in the previous answer. (The tribunal would probably have hit on that idea, but your suggesting it could save time.) You would need to provide evidence that the U.S. tribunal really is the forum wherein the proofs are best collected, as might be the case, for example, if several of the witnesses who know the details of the marriage also live in the U.S.

The American tribunal would still need the consent of the judicial vicar of wherever your ex-spouse has canonical domicile, and neither you nor the tribunal can force that consent. I have seen many such requests granted, however, based on the fact that Third World tribunals do not enjoy making petitioners wait three to five years for a decision, which often is the situation in marriage nullity cases. There is no requirement that your former spouse live in the territory of the same episcopal conference that you do.

Confusion on this point might have led whomever you consulted to say that your nullity petition had to be heard in the country wherein your ex-wife still lives.

If the forum of proofs approach fails, you could consider approaching the Supreme Tribunal of the Apostolic Signatura in the Vatican for *prorogation*— that is, transfer—of competence to a tribunal more convenient to you. Such permissions are not commonly granted, especially when the foreign tribunal is willing to accept the case, but neither are they unheard of. Seek canonical advice before attempting to contact the Signatura.

You could, of course, file your case in your home country. It may be slower (see canon 1453, suggesting one year as the basic time limit on deciding cases), but at least you would be in the system somewhere.

Question 22: **Can I file my nullity petition in Rome?**

Yes (1983 CIC 1417 § 1, 1444), but why would you want to? It is almost certainly going to be slower, more expensive, and generally more cumbersome than proceeding in a local tribunal. Besides, if you are not satisfied with the results of the local tribunal process, you still have the right to appeal to Rome (1983 CIC 1628).

Question 23: **If I move away after filing my nullity petition, will the tribunal still hear the case?**

Probably, especially if the tribunal has formally accepted the case and cited the respondent since it has probably acquired jurisdiction over the case (1983 CIC 1512, n. 2). On the other hand, if you anticipate moving rather soon after filing your nullity case, you should tell the tribunal about that because your absence could make the investigation of the case more difficult. It could even be to your advantage to hold off filing your petition until you reach your new diocese. If you do move during the process, though, there are means of having your case transferred to a more convenient but still competent diocesan tribunal, generally by "renouncing" your first filing under canon 1524.

Question 24: **Will I have to appear for an interview if I file a nullity petition?**

As the petitioner, you should certainly be prepared and willing to appear, but you will not necessarily be called (1983 CIC 1530, 1528). Although tribunals vary in their approaches, many tend to schedule interviews only if there are serious ambiguities that require resolution prior to sentence. Sometimes petitioner and respondent declarations are so clear and detailed in themselves, and enjoy such credible support from witnesses, that the tribunal can reach a decision (whether affirmative or negative) based on them (see also 1983 CIC 1606, expressly allowing for a speedy decision in such cases). Likewise, the *instruction* of the case might reveal a failure to observe canonical form or an undispensed impediment, eliminating the need for a formal trial (1983 CIC 1686).

Often, however, there are conflicts or discrepancies in testimony or significant gaps in the narration. In such cases the tribunal is more likely to call for an interview with either or both parties. Sometimes witnesses too are asked to supplement their testimony, either in writing or by means of an interview.

Question 25: **Since filing my petition for nullity, I guess you could say I've had second thoughts. Can I cancel the case?**

Assuming the case has not already been decided, you as the petitioner can probably stop the proceedings.

First, under canon 1524, you could notify the tribunal in writing of your desire to "renounce the instance." Your request for renunciation of the case is then communicated to the respondent, who is allowed a brief (but canonically unspecified) period in which to accept, or at least not oppose, your request. If this period passes uneventfully, the judge is then authorized (and probably required, but the Code of Canon Law is not clear on this point) to accept the renunciation. If the respondent objects to your request, the judge again is authorized to decide whatever he thinks is best.

In my experience, virtually all requests for renunciation are granted. Tribunals have more than enough to do deciding cases in which people want answers without deciding cases in which people do not want answers.

(Note: For the respondent who still wishes the case to go forward despite the petitioner's renunciation, my advice would be to state your objections to the renunciation and, if the renunciation is granted— as it probably will be—turn around and become the petitioner in a new filing. Your former spouse cannot stop you from filing your own petition in accord with canon law.)

Generally, petitioners who renounce the instance are free to reopen their petition upon request at a later time. This happens, for example, in cases where renunciation was requested and granted because witnesses failed to come forward on the case, but with the passage of time (and the healing of feelings?) they decide to cooperate. In such cases it is the right of the tribunal to seek updating of already submitted depositions and testimony, lest petitioners simply submit time-sensitive materials when it suits them, regardless of their usefulness to the tribunal.

The second, rather riskier, way to stop a case is simply to fail to respond to the tribunal's communications for six months (1983 CIC 1520). This is called *abatement* and is meant to give tribunals a way out of deciding cases in which the parties seem to have lost interest in the outcome even if they do not actually say so. But, as is always true whenever intentions are gleaned from lack of action, confusion can arise with abatement. This is especially true for respondents, since their failure to respond to tribunal inquiries could be taken as contempt, and their silence, as it were, held against them (1983 CIC 1531 § 2, 1592, 1595). Moreover, the mere fact that one has not heard from the tribunal for over six months does not necessarily mean that the case is abated. It could simply be tribunal backlog at work.

If a petitioner really wishes to stop a case from going forward, the canons on renunciation should be followed.

CHAPTER 4

WHEN AN ANNULMENT
MIGHT BE NEEDED

Question 26: **I already have a civil divorce, but I have been told that I also need an annulment before getting married in Church again. Is this so?**

You have been advised correctly. A civil divorce (or for that matter, a civil annulment) does nothing to affect one's presumed marital status in the Church. Canon 1401, n. 1, states that the Church alone adjudicates cases dealing with spiritual matters, such as annulment petitions, and canon 1671 adds that the marriage nullity cases of all the baptized (not just Catholics) can be treated under canon law. In the United States, civil law does not recognize ecclesiastical annulments; the Catholic Church does not recognize civil divorces anywhere.

Question 27: **Please explain one thing for me. Long before I was Catholic, I was married and divorced, and then I remarried and have been blessed with many years of happiness ever since. I am planning to enter the Church, but there is all this concern about my first marriage. I understand that Catholics are not allowed to divorce, and I will not get divorced as a Catholic. But why should that first marriage from my non-Catholic days be of such concern? It was over years ago. I feel as if I'm now being held to rules that didn't apply to me then.**

Another, if perhaps blunter, way of putting your question would be to ask whether the Church accepts the validity of non-Catholic marriages. Good heavens, I hope it does, and in fact the Church does presume the validity of non-Catholic marriages. At the risk of some oversimplification, anything that more or less looks like a marriage among non-Catholics is going to be presumed by the Church to have been a marriage and hence worthy of the respect due marriage. What you are being held to is not so much the Church's law on marriage but what the Church considers to be God's law on marriage. In most cases that implies permanence (lasting till death) and exclusivity (having only one spouse) in marriage (reflected in, but not derived from, 1983 CIC 1056).

But maybe you still do not see the difference? Try this: Canonical form, for example, is a creation of ecclesiastical law and applies only to Catholics. You are not being held to canonical form—meaning, by the way, that you cannot use canonical form issues to impugn your non-Catholic wedding, although the Church generally expects some type of religious or civil wedding ceremony between non-Catholics. On the other hand, basic matrimonial capacity and consent issues, based at least in part on divine or natural law, could bind even non-Catholics and hence could be used as the basis for challenging a non-Catholic marriage.

Thus, whatever kind of first marriage you went through seems to meet the very minimal requirements for a presumably valid, albeit non-Catholic marriage, and hence, for as long as your former spouse is alive, the Church will consider you bound by that first marriage unless and until its nullity is proven in accord with canon law.

Question 28: **After my divorce, I got married again. That was several years ago. I am now hoping to come into the Church. Will I need an annulment of my first marriage, and if it's granted, will I need to get married again in the Church?**

Assuming your first spouse is still alive (and assuming that things like the *Pauline Privilege* do not apply in your case), then yes, you will need to have your first marriage assessed in a formal nullity case, and your petition might result in an annulment. As to your need to undergo another marriage upon entering the Church, however, that is another matter. Catholics are bound to observe the laws of the Church and in a special way the canons concerning marriage. That law, for all the obvious reasons, prohibits Catholics from entering second marriages while the first spouse is still alive (1983 CIC 1085 § 1). Therefore, Catholics who have gone through any kind of marriage ceremony should not, even after a civil divorce, attempt another marriage until the status of that first marriage has been adjudicated by an ecclesiastical court. This rule applies even when it seems perfectly obvious that the first attempt at marriage was null (1983 CIC 1085 § 2). There are several reasons for this rule. First, what looked like a null marriage might, upon qualified examination, be shown to be, if not valid (for no marriage can ever be proven valid), at least worthy of the presumption of validity. Only a tribunal—not the parties involved, not pastors, not spiritual advisors—can make this kind of technical determination. Second, family and friends can be scandalized or just plain confused by private parties determining for themselves which of their marriages ought to be valid and which ones should not. Only the action of a qualified institution such as the diocesan tribunal can answer their unspoken questions and alleviate unvoiced concerns. Finally, the Church as a community has an interest in keeping track of who is married to whom, and this cannot be accomplished if its members feel free to enter and leave marriages whenever they choose.

If you have been Catholic all along, and your second marriage took place outside the Church (that is, canonical form was not observed), then, even if your first marriage was later proven to be null, you will still not be considered married in the eyes of the Church until your second marriage is *convalidated* (1983 CIC 1056) or, as many people call it, "blessed in the Church." In very unusual circumstances, your second marriage could even be *radically sanated* (1983 CIC 1161, 1165). This is similar to a convalidation but does not include a renewal of consent.

On the other hand, if you and your second spouse were not Catholic at the time of your second marriage—and hence not bound by canonical form—then your second marriage is automatically going to be considered valid by the Church effective from the date you entered that second marriage, upon proof that the first marriage was invalid. An example of this potentially confusing point might help.

Two baptized non-Catholics marry and divorce. One of them marries again and later wishes to enter the Church. The fact of having two apparent marriages is an obstacle to full communion, right? So an annulment petition on the first marriage is filed. Assuming grounds for nullity are identified and canonically proven, then that first marriage is null. This means that at the time the spouse entered the second marriage, Church law considered him or her free to marry. Not being Catholic and hence not bound by canonical form, the person's second marriage is presumed to be valid. Such a person, then, is already considered married under canon law, and upon reception into the Church, he or she need not convalidate the marriage.

Question 29: **My former husband and I were married in a Catholic ceremony. We divorced several years later, and I did not remarry. About one year ago, he died. I've wondered many times over the years if our marriage was really valid, and just for my own peace of mind, I'd like to know. My pastor, however, has told me that the tribunal will not hear a marriage case after one of the spouses dies. Is that correct?**

Your pastor is correct. Canon 1675 § 1 states that a marriage that has not been impugned while both spouses were still alive cannot be impugned after the death of either or both spouses. The only exception to this rule would be if the question of the validity of the marriage were important to the resolution of some other canonical or civil question.

Question 30: **I was married in the Church, and later divorced. I remarried outside of the Church, and have remained married since then. I admit that this marriage is invalid in the Church's eyes. Recently, I learned that my ex-spouse had died. My question is: If I want to get my marriage blessed in the Church, do I still need to have an annulment of my first marriage?**

No, because the death of your first spouse releases you from the bond of marriage, which as you seem to see correctly, the Church presumes to have arisen from your first marriage. I would only note that the mere death of your former spouse does not "validate," as it were, your second marriage (assuming it took place before the death of your former spouse). You do need to renew your consent to marriage in what canon law calls a *convalidation* but what most people simply refer to as "having a marriage blessed in the Church" (see 1983 CIC 1156, 1160).

Question 31: **As a result of a very complicated set of facts surrounding an unresolved accident my wife had several years ago, the civil courts declared her dead, even though we never recovered her body. I am getting conflicting opinions on whether I need an annulment before getting married again. Please advise.**

I can imagine you are getting differing stories. This is an unusual case.

If you received a certificate of death, then the mere fact that a body was not recovered (as might happen, say, in a ship sinking or an earthquake) does not negate the fact that the certain death of one spouse ended the bond of marriage for the surviving spouse. If, on the other hand, the spouse's absence is due to something like a "missing and presumed dead" situation (say, the ship sank, but there are reasonable questions as to whether the spouse was actually on the ship), or if the spouse has simply disappeared for an extended period of time, then the Church is going to consider the "surviving" spouse bound by the marriage unless one of three things happens: (1) the other spouse is actually located, living or deceased, and the matter is handled accordingly; (2) the marriage is annulled using the regular laws on annulment, including those on proceeding in case of an absent respondent; or (3) the diocesan bishop, after a thorough investigation, canonically decrees the presumed death of the missing spouse (1983 CIC 1707).

As mentioned above, the mere absence of the spouse, even for many years, and even if civil law regards him or her as dead, does not allow a bishop to decree that spouse dead. There has to be some evidence of actual death.

If a spouse is decreed "presumed dead" according to canon 1707, the other spouse is considered canonically free to marry in the Church. But if the original spouse is alive, the second marriage is null, even though it was entered into in the best of faith by both parties. If there are, therefore, legitimate grounds to petition the nullity of the marriage, and if sufficient evidence of nullity can be offered, it is probably more prudent to consider such a process before resorting to a "presumed death" procedure.

Question 32: **My husband and I were married in a Catholic ceremony, and later we divorced, but we did not seek an annulment. We recently reconciled and remarried each other before a justice of the peace. Do we need to have our first marriage annulled, and then be remarried by a priest?**

No. Marriages celebrated in the Church are presumed valid until a Church court declares them otherwise (1983 CIC 1060). Your civil divorce did nothing to change things from the Church's point of view. There is, therefore, no requirement that you either file for an annulment of your "first" marriage, or that you "renew" your vows.

Question 33: **I've been divorced for several years and have no intention of remarrying. In fact, I've been thinking about applying for admission to a religious order. I will certainly tell them about my marriage and divorce, but is there a chance I might have to apply for an annulment even to join religious life?**

Yes, there is a very good chance you will (1983 CIC 643 1, n. 2). The same applies if you are considering entrance into a secular institute (1983 CIC 721 § 1, n. 3) or society of apostolic life (1983 CIC 735 2) to say nothing of some forms of holy orders (1983 CIC 277, 1041, n.1). Dispensations that would allow a canonically married (even if civilly divorced) person to enter consecrated life or certain forms of holy orders are sometimes possible, but they are unlikely if the annulment process has not been tried first.

CHAPTER 5

QUESTIONS ON ELIGIBILITY TO FILE ANNULMENT CASES

Question 34: **May the spouse who filed for the divorce also file for the annulment?**

Yes. For a long time in Church law, the fact of having filed for a civil divorce could be considered evidence of being "responsible" for the breakup of the marriage. Since the early 1970s, however, canonical restrictions that prevented "guilty" spouses from submitting their marriage nullity cases have been dropped. Today, therefore, it makes little difference, canonically or practically, whether the petitioner or the respondent filed for the civil divorce.

Question 35: **Is a civil divorce necessary before filing for an annulment?**

Virtually every diocesan tribunal in America requires proof of a civil divorce before accepting a canonical nullity petition. The reason usually given for such a policy is, however, quite unsatisfying: Many tribunals apparently fear that they can be sued by irate spouses for "alienation of affection" if they accept a nullity petition before there is a civil divorce between the parties. Now, in this day in which no legal theory is too novel for some civil court somewhere to accept, I cannot say that such a fear is utterly groundless. Today one can be sued civilly for almost anything. But remember that annulments in the United

States have no civil effects—they are purely exercises in religious rights motivated by theological beliefs. This reality, in my opinion, deserves some respect by civil courts for all sorts of weighty constitutional reasons. Do not get me wrong: I do not think Catholic dioceses should go around looking for fights with secular courts. But neither do I think they should be forced to curb their important ecclesial operations merely to suit some civil lawyer's theory of state power over churches. Do I hold, therefore, that the "divorce before annulment requirement" is a bad idea? No. If nothing else, a civil divorce is a practical way of determining that there is no realistic hope of reconciling the parties, something tribunal judges are required to verify as part of every tribunal case, marriage-related or otherwise (1983 CIC 1676).

The "divorce before annulment requirement" works in the great majority of cases, and if one is planning to remarry, a civil divorce is going to be necessary anyway. But if for unusual reasons a civil divorce cannot be procured, that fact by itself should not be held sufficient to reject a petitioner's *libellus* (1983 CIC 1505 § 2). In case of serious disputes over this point with your diocesan tribunal, you should seek independent canonical advice.

Question 36: I am not planning to marry again, but since my divorce I have sometimes wondered whether I should apply for an annulment. Am I eligible to apply even if I am not planning to remarry?

Your intention, or your lack of intention, to marry again is irrelevant to your right to petition for an annulment. Although many people do not apply for an annulment until they are considering entering (or are already in) another marriage, many others do petition for a declaration of nullity just for their own peace of mind. Generally, there is some advantage to the petitioner (and respondent) in filing a nullity petition sooner rather than later. Memories are fresher and usually more accurate. Witnesses are still available, documents are easier to find, and so on. Every tribunal judge has seen marriage nullity cases in which plausible grounds for nullity were put forward but that fail because the long period that passed between the time of the marriage and the time of filing the nullity petition made it impossible to prove the petitioner's claims.

Sometimes there is a second advantage to filing marriage nullity cases sooner rather than later: namely, the personally beneficial effects of going through a process that requires an honest, dispassionate review of a traumatic experience. Every tribunal judge knows of people who said that the divorce did little to close the books on a traumatic marriage, but that the tribunal process was a great help in that regard.

Question 37: **My divorce was some time ago, and for a long time I had no intention of ever getting married again. Now I have met someone and we are engaged. I'm willing to file for an annulment, but I wonder whether I should say anything about being engaged. Will that not look bad to them?**

Since your intentions regarding remarriage are, strictly speaking, irrelevant to your right to file a petition of nullity, there is no reason to hide the fact of your engagement. Indeed, there seems some risk of raising questions about your frankness with the tribunal if you hide the fact and it finds out from other sources, which often happens. Most tribunals will ask you about potential marriage plans anyway, and actual deception regarding this fact can be held against you. Even then, such deception is probably not enough to scuttle your nullity petition, since marriage nullity cases ultimately turn upon different issues.

In reality, most petitioners in tribunal cases are either already remarried or hoping to remarry in the near future. Your hopes or plans to remarry place you, therefore, in a big and canonically inconspicuous boat; any deception by you on this point, however, would place you in a small and very conspicuous boat.

When diocesan tribunals ask about future marriage plans, it is usually for one of three reasons:

1) If there are plans for a wedding, the tribunal will go out of its way to explain timetables and potential problems that might interfere with those marriage plans. This is to protect you or others from surprise and disappointment if things do not work out. For example, your annulment might not be declared, or if it is declared, a prohibition against future marriage might be imposed.

2) The tribunal might wish to do a preliminary assessment of the eligibility of the prospective spouse to enter marriage in the Church, lest there be problems with his or her freedom to marry.

3) If the intended spouse had a role in the breakup of the first marriage, the tribunal had better hear about it from you rather than from your ex-spouse or witnesses. Although adultery is no longer an impediment to future marriage, as it was under the 1917 Code (see 1917 CIC 1075, n. 1), it is still an important piece of information for the tribunal to have as it attempts to determine matrimonial capacity and consent at the time of the previous wedding.

Question 38: **I think my marriage was null, but I cannot go in there and claim that I never loved my former wife because I did love her. I can't say that there weren't any good times together because there were. I know it, she knows it, and God knows it. Should I even bother to file for annulment?**

Whether you file for an annulment is up to you, and whether your petition is accepted and eventually granted would be up to the tribunal system acting in accord with canon law. But having loved your former spouse and having shared good times together is no more a bar to your filing a nullity petition than having failed to love your spouse and never having shared any good times together would be sufficient to grant your petition. While love and happy memories are more likely in healthy marriages, they are not, strictly speaking, the kinds of things that nullity cases are decided upon. As I have said many times, all nullity cases turn upon, and only upon, issues related to capacity, consent, and form. Love and happy experiences, or the lack thereof, might shed some light on the kinds of issues that concern tribunals, but they are not themselves the issues upon which tribunals decide cases.

Question 39: **After my divorce, I fell away from the Church. Actually, I haven't been in a church for over fifteen years. If I wanted to have my marriage reviewed for the possibility of an annulment, would my lengthy absence from the Catholic Church be held against me? I would understand if it did, but I was wondering anyway.**

The failure to practice one's faith is a serious matter, of course, but it would not prevent you filing a marriage petition, nor would it be grounds for the tribunal to reject your petition. The scenario you describe is not uncommon, and often enough an annulment is part of one's return to the practice of the faith.

Question 40: **My husband and I have been happily married for over thirty years in the Presbyterian Church. After several years of prayer and study I have decided to become Catholic. My husband does not object, but he has no interest in joining the Catholic Church himself. He was briefly married and divorced before he and I ever met. I've been told that this is an obstacle to my entering the Catholic Church, but that if his first marriage were annulled, we would be considered validly married for Catholic purposes, and I would be free to enter the Church. My problem is that my husband has no interest in asking for a Catholic annulment. I've been told that I am not eligible to file a case for him. What can I do, if anything, to clear this up?**

Your question is complicated, but it is not unheard of. It is probable that such situations are going to be encountered more frequently as Catholic evangelism efforts toward Protestant denominations result in the conversion of one canonically free-to-marry spouse, while the other spouse has a matrimonial history that he or she has no interest in resolving to the Church's satisfaction. The canonical problem, as you have experienced, is that you have no power to impugn the former marriage of your current spouse that is preventing your entry into the Church (1983 CIC 1674).

There are, however, a couple ways of approaching things. First, you should ask your husband whether he is willing to file a nullity petition in his own name, even if, as you say, he has no interest in the outcome. Perhaps putting him in touch with someone who can explain the situation to him better than you would be helpful. It might take time, but some people in your husband's position eventually decide to cooperate, if only for the sake of the spouse for whom this process is important.

If you have tried this to no avail, there is another way of impugning a marriage. It involves a tribunal official known as the *Promoter of Justice*. The Promoter is the one other person who can impugn a marriage, at least under certain circumstances. The procedure I am about to describe is very unusual, but it is quite within the law.

Under canon 1674, n. 2, the Promoter of Justice can impugn a marriage if the nullity of the marriage has become widely known and the marriage cannot be *convalidated* (in effect, repaired), or at least such is not expedient. Before explaining these terms, it is important to realize canon 1674 notably increases the authority of Promoters to impugn marriages over what they used to enjoy under the 1917 Code.

Under the 1917 Code, the Promoter of Justice could impugn a marriage only if it was invalid due to an impediment, and only an impediment that was by its nature canonically public (1917 CIC 1971 1, n. 2). Thus, under the 1917 Code, the Promoter could impugn a marriage based on, for example, *nonage* (that is, extreme youth). Insufficient age at the time of a wedding is an impediment and moreover one that can be proven in the external forum by documents such as birth certificates. But, under the 1917 Code, if the marriage was invalid because of *nonpublic impediments* or because of a failure to give proper consent, or because canonical form was not correctly followed, there was nothing the Promoter could do about it, and the marriage could be impugned only by one of the two parties to it. The situation such as the one you describe, therefore, could not be addressed under the 1917 Code.

The 1983 Code, however, reads very differently on this point. No longer is the Promoter of Justice limited to impugning only marriages that are invalid based on public impediments. Now *any* grounds of nullity can be argued by the Promoter, including failures of consent and improper canonical form. Nor is there any requirement that the grounds of nullity proposed by the Promoter be canonically public. Of course, the Promoter must still prove his case against the marriage, but at least now he is authorized to present it to the diocesan tribunal for consideration.

The only current restrictions on the authority of the Promoter of Justice to impugn a marriage are that the nullity of the marriage must be "divulged"—that is, made known—and that convalidation of that marriage must be impossible or at least inexpedient. The Code does not define these conditions further, but a good case can be made that a marriage that ended in divorce several decades earlier can be said to be widely regarded as null. This is especially true if it was the type of marriage that is more easily proven null. Further, when the parties have gone on to other marriages, often producing children of their own and perhaps losing all contact with each other, the case can likewise be made that trying to convalidate the earlier marriage is, to put it mildly, inexpedient. The situation you describe seems to meet several, perhaps all, of these criteria, and it is certainly worth considering if your husband still declines to enter a case in his own name.

Do not be put off if you are told, "We don't do those here," or "They are too complicated for our tribunal," when you suggest a Promoter of Justice case. Most Promoters have not been involved in such a case before, and they might be reluctant to attempt one. On the other hand, the law is there to be used, and it has been reformed to make it easier to use. Granted, there are some technical issues beyond the scope of this book that have to ironed out in particular cases, but a good canon lawyer should be able to assist you.

Canon 1752, in a sort of offhand manner, closes the 1983 Code of Canon Law by stating that canonical equity and the salvation of souls are always the supreme law of the Church. The situation you describe surely merits consideration from both points of view.

Question 41: **I know this might sound strange, but here goes. I'm divorced but I'm not Catholic. Neither was my ex. I'm not planning to join the Catholic Church, but I am thinking about getting married again (not to a Catholic, by the way). The Protestant denomination I belong to does not have an annulment process like yours. They feel that a civil divorce is sufficient. I don't feel completely comfortable with their position. Would it be possible to have your people take a case like mine, and tell me what they thought about it?**

First, you are free to seek informal opinions on your first marriage from anybody you like, and the quality of the opinions you get would depend on the knowledge and good sense of your advisors and on the accuracy of the information you share. But you seem to be asking something more—namely, whether you can actually submit a nullity petition to a diocesan tribunal and get a formal decision from it, even if you are not canonically bound by that decision. The answer to that question is yes, you can submit your petition to a Catholic tribunal (1983 CIC 1476) and receive a formal sentence. The canonical restrictions against non-Catholics approaching diocesan tribunals with cases have been lifted, more or less, since shortly after the Second Vatican Council, and canon law expressly asserts the right of the Church to adjudicate the marriage nullity cases of *all* baptized persons, Catholic or not (1983 CIC 1671, 1055 § 2, 1400, 1401). Admittedly, most of the nullity petitions that diocesan tribunals receive from non-Catholics are prompted by the desire of one (or both) of the parties to enter the Church or to marry a Catholic, but neither condition is a requirement for filing a nullity petition.

You would have to meet all the same procedural requirements as other people, of course, and pay your share of the expenses. Moreover, as far as the Church is concerned, your petition would be adjudicated. If you ever were to consider entering the Church or marrying a Catholic, the results of your case would be relevant.

Question 42: **Since our divorce, my ex and I have remained on pretty decent terms. I was wondering if perhaps we could file for an annulment of our marriage together, so that neither one of us comes across as attacking the other.**

Canon law, like most legal systems, generally allows only one person to be the petitioner and one person to be the respondent. Unlike most other legal systems, however, canon law does not pit one side against the other, even though there is often some feeling that this is being done. Even if the parties to a canonical case disagree as to how the case should be resolved, canon law does not, strictly speaking, see them as opposed to each other. Rather it sees two competing theories about how to resolve a problem, neither of which theory necessarily binds the tribunal, which must always act in accord with law. In most cases, it is very quickly evident to the tribunal what kind of "terms" the parties maintain with each other.

If it is important to you and your ex-spouse not to come across as trying to antagonize each other, then whichever of you decides to be the petitioner could include in the petition a letter from the other spouse saying something like, "I look forward to cooperating in this case." But it is really not necessary.

Question 43: **I was married and divorced many years ago, and I received an annulment of that first marriage. Then I remarried and stayed married until a few years ago, when my second husband left me. We divorced, of course, and I'm ambivalent about ever getting married again. But just in case, would the fact that I already got one annulment prevent me from applying for another?**

There is no canonical restriction on the number of times one can apply for an annulment. Lest that sound like Church approval for "serial marriages," however, remember that canon 1077 allows the diocesan tribunal to prohibit future marriages in the Church for serious reasons. Propensity toward serial marriage would, I think, certainly qualify as serious reason. Your question does not suggest that kind of thinking, but I mention it anyway.

Question 44: **My ex-spouse and I were married first by a justice of the peace. After a few years, when things weren't going so well, we decided to get married in the Church, thinking that maybe it would help our marriage. It didn't, and we are now divorced. Will the fact that we went through two ceremonies be held against us? Are we still eligible to apply for annulment even though we got married in the Church?**

Your question implies that you and probably your former spouse were both Catholic, hence you both probably disregarded canonical form in attempting your civil marriage. This will not be "held against" you, and indeed your civil marriage shows that neither you nor your spouse had much regard for (or understanding of) the Church's teaching on marriage. Moreover, your "second" wedding (really, your first as far as the Church is concerned) does not prevent you from filing a nullity petition, and many marriage nullity cases deal with exactly these kinds of situations. In a sense, though, your second ceremony complicates things. Had you been able to bring to the tribunal only a civil wedding, such a petition probably would have been identified as a *defect of form* case and thus be eligible for an expedited hearing under canon 1686. Almost certainly, such a petition would be easily proven and quickly declared. But in having a canonical wedding (assuming that is what you did when you say you married in the Church), you have forced the tribunal to investigate the more complex questions about matrimonial capacity and consent at the time of the second wedding. The nullity of your first, civil attempt at marriage is clear, but the tribunal will also have to investigate formally your second, canonical ceremony. Thus, it will be important for the parties and witnesses in the case to speak about the second ceremony as well as the first.

Often enough, of course, the same factors that led a couple into a civil wedding are seriously damaging to basic matrimonial capacity and consent at the time of the ecclesiastical ceremony. Your case is not an unusual one, and it has been made, ironically, more complicated by your having made some effort to be faithful to the Church's laws on marriage.

Question 45: **Before our wedding, we had a formal engagement blessing, the kind you don't see much anymore. Will the fact that we underwent that additional ceremony prevent either of us from filing for an annulment after our divorce is final?**

The delightful ceremony you refer to is not in common use these days, although it is still available (more or less under 1983 CIC 1063, n. 2). To answer your question, though—no, the fact that you and your former spouse underwent an engagement ceremony does not prevent you from filing a petition of nullity in regard to that marriage. Indeed, after such a ceremony, the parties remain canonically free not to marry (1983 CIC 1062 § 2). The most that could be said about the engagement ceremony would be that it might be evidence that you and your former spouse were, at the time of the wedding, apparently taking additional steps to prepare well for marriage.

CHAPTER 6

POSSIBLE GROUNDS FOR AN ANNULMENT

Question 46: I have been told there are "multiple grounds" in my marriage case. What are "grounds," multiple or otherwise?

"Grounds" in an annulment case are like "causes of action" in a civil case or "counts" in a criminal case. The grounds in an annulment case are the reasons why one or both parties to a marriage assert that their marriage is null. Like civil causes of action or criminal counts, the mere assertion of grounds for nullity does not automatically result in nullity being declared. Grounds still have to be recognized in law and then proven (1983 CIC 1526). Broadly speaking, there are six ways any marriage might be proven null. First and second, it could be shown that either the husband or the wife lacked basic capacity for marriage. Third and fourth, it could be shown that either the husband or the wife did not give sufficiently his or her consent to marriage as the Church understands and proclaims it. Fifth and sixth, it could be shown that either the husband or the wife failed to manifest this consent in a proper way. None of these categories is mutually exclusive of any other category, and so two or more of them could be present in a particular case, thus presenting multiple grounds for nullity.

If you have been told that there are multiple grounds for nullity in your case, it is because the tribunal has identified, or is at least investigating, more than one specific basis for nullity. Let's take an example.

Suppose a fifteen-year-old Catholic boy was forced at gunpoint to marry a fifteen-year-old pregnant Catholic girl before a justice of the peace. Such a case offers several grounds for nullity. Assuming there was evidence to prove each of the above parts of the story, this marriage could be declared null on any or all of the following grounds:

1) lack of age for the boy (canon 1083 requires Catholic men to be at least sixteen years old before marrying, although Catholic girls can validly marry at fourteen);

2) force and grave fear used against the boy (1983 CIC 1103);

3) complete lack of canonical form on the part of the boy (canons 1108 and 1117 requires the Catholic boy to marry in a Catholic ceremony);

4) complete lack of canonical form on the part of the girl (canons 1108 and 1117 also require Catholic girls to marry in a Catholic ceremony).

Any one of these grounds, standing completely alone, is sufficient to declare the marriage null. For that matter, other grounds for nullity could be considered as well. For example, canon 1095, n.2, requires that those entering marriage be able to exercise adequate discretion of judgment upon entering marriage. A very good case could be made that teenage boys (even those over age fifteen) and pregnant teenage girls (even if they are over fourteen) do not usually exercise adequate discretion of judgment in entering any kind of marriage, let alone "shotgun" marriages.

Not every case, however, that offers multiple grounds for nullity is actually adjudicated on each of those grounds.

In the above example, it would probably be a waste of time for the diocesan tribunal to adjudicate the issues related to canon 1095, that can be rather complex, when the "open-and-shut" grounds of nonage and lack of form are available. Since nullity of *any* type, in *either* party, results in nullity of the whole marriage, multiple grounds tend to be adjudicated only if those additional issues are necessary for the treatment of something besides nullity—say, in helping the tribunal address the question of imposing a restriction (either *monitum* or *vetitum*) on future marriage on either or both parties.

This is important to understand for another reason: The mere fact that grounds were "joined" (that is, heard) on just one party does not necessarily imply that grounds could not have also been joined on the other party. It could simply mean that the quantity and quality of the evidence concerning the first party were more than enough to reach moral certitude of the nullity of the marriage. Likewise, the fact that the tribunal declared nullity on the basis of one capacity, consent, or form issue does not mean that there were not other issues seriously affecting the marriage. It just means that such additional issues, if they existed, were not needed to prove the nullity of the marriage.

Question 47: Is pregnancy at the time of the wedding grounds for an annulment?

No. Pregnancy at the time of marriage (or, for that matter, premarital sex) is not an impediment to marriage. Therefore, all things being equal, persons in these circumstances still have the canonical capacity to marry. Nevertheless, premarital sex and resulting pregnancies can, in some cases, adversely affect the consent of the parties to a marriage. For all the reasons the Church has untiringly explained, premarital sex is not a good preparation for

Christian marriage. Pregnancy, moreover, can bring with it additional physical, emotional, and financial issues that might interfere with the prayer, planning, and honest reflection that ought to be part of the marriage decision process. These additional factors can impair one's ability to deliberate and choose freely, sometimes resulting in a wedding that is a reaction to circumstances rather than a manifestation of the couple's sufficient commitment to Christian marriage. If the tribunal determines that the stressors of pregnancy and related factors were such as to preclude sufficient consent to marriage as the Church understands and proclaims it, nullity can be declared.

Question 48: **My wife had a two-month affair with one of the men where she works. Is her infidelity grounds for an annulment?**

Infidelity is a serious violation of the exclusive unity between husband and wife, which is an essential property of marriage (1983 CIC 1056). Objectively, infidelity is gravely sinful, and it qualifies as a basis for *canonical separation* (see 1983 CIC 1151, 1155). Infidelity is not, however, grounds for an annulment. Standing alone, it does not prove the failure of matrimonial capacity, consent, or form at the time of the wedding, proof of which is required in every annulment case. Under certain circumstances, though, infidelity also might be evidence (though not complete proof) that another condition is present and was present at the time of the wedding, a condition so destructive of matrimonial capacity or consent that it could serve as the basis for an annulment (see, for example, 1983 CIC 1095 or 1101). In such a case, however, it is the alleged lack of capacity for or failure of consent to marriage in the first place that must be proven with moral certitude, and not merely the fact of post-wedding infidelity.

Question 49: Is my ex-spouse's alcoholism grounds for an annulment?

Alcoholism, whether as a professionally verified condition or, more generically, as a pattern of life with fairly obvious and consistent signs, is not a canonical impediment to marriage (see 1983 CIC 1083, 1094) and cannot therefore serve as the basis upon which nullity is declared. On the other hand, active, unaddressed alcoholism is obviously a very serious condition which, upon verification, could show that, at the time of the wedding, either or both parties could not assume the essential obligations of married life for reasons of a psychic nature (*causas naturae psychicae*) as described in canon 1095, n. 3. This, in turn, could be the basis of nullity in such a marriage. This is not just a word game. It needs to be repeated that mere demonstration of alcoholism is not and cannot be, under canon law as it currently reads, a basis for matrimonial nullity. Consider the fact that most reformed or recovering alcoholics describe themselves as alcoholics. One should not conclude, however, that such people as a class are incapable of marriage. Active alcoholism that does not manifest itself until several years into a marriage is less likely to serve as the basis of nullity under canon 1095, n. 3. Still the petitioner (or the respondent, for that matter) would be allowed to introduce evidence that the same factors that contributed to the later active alcoholism also prevented the assumption of matrimonial obligations at the time of the wedding. This involves a higher burden of proof, if you will, but it could be argued.

By the way, many tribunals require the testimony of an expert in hearing cases under canon 1095, n. 3, but there are some cases whose fact patterns are so patent and so grave that the calling of an expert would be superfluous (1983 CIC 1574). Moreover, everything said in answer to this question about alcoholism would probably apply in cases of any chemical addiction.

In cases in which one does not claim or cannot prove active drug addiction or alcoholism in a clinical sense of the term, evidence of chronic drug and alcohol abuse is often relevant to one or both parties' levels of maturity and discretion of judgment in entering marriage—that is, in cases turning upon canon 1095, n. 2. Finally, it is possible that drug or alcohol abuse or addiction could be used as evidence of other types of canonical nullity, for example, *simulation* (1983 CIC 1101).

Question 50: **When I got married, I needed to get a dispensation because my ex-husband was not baptized. I got the dispensation, but later we were divorced and we've gone our separate ways. I've been thinking about applying for annulment, and someone told me it would be an easier case because my marriage was not a sacrament. I don't understand this because we were married in a Catholic church by a Catholic priest.**

It is true that a marriage between a Christian, even a Catholic, and an unbaptized person is not a sacrament (1983 CIC 1055 2), but it is still presumed to be a *valid* marriage and hence benefits from all of the canons that uphold marriage (1983 CIC 1060 and others). The fact that you received the necessary dispensation from the impediment of *disparity of cult* (1983 CIC 1086 § 1) also supports that presumption. Despite its being a non-sacramental marriage, your case still must meet all the canonical requirements that face other nullity petitions in diocesan tribunals. It will be neither easier nor harder to adjudicate. By the way, there is some chance that your case could also be considered as a "Favor of the Faith" case, which is different from a Pauline Privilege situation. Favor of the Faith cases are heard only in Rome, even though they are prepared by the local tribunal. An explanation of them is beyond the scope of this work, but you might ask your tribunal about them. They will probably be able to tell you very quickly if you are eligible.

Question 51: **My former spouse has filed for an annulment, and I believe he is planning to use my infertility, which we did not know about before our wedding, as the basis of his annulment. I feel this is terribly unfair. Please advise.**

While your former spouse is basically allowed to suggest the basis, or "grounds," for an annulment case (1983 CIC 1504, n. 2), he cannot dictate the grounds to the tribunal, which retains the right and duty to decide upon what basis the case will be heard (1983 CIC 1513). In any event, infertility—as opposed, say, to impotence or frigidity (1983 CIC 1084)—is not a canonical basis for nullity. If it is the sole basis upon which your former spouse can try to impugn your marriage, the petition will fail, assuming it is even accepted, which is not likely (1983 CIC 1505 § 2, n. 4). By the way, the situation described above is different from a case where one spouse *refuses* to have children. If this intention was present at the time of the wedding, and can be demonstrated to the tribunal, it may be considered as grounds for impugning the validity of the marriage.

Question 52: **Our wedding was not celebrated in a Mass. Is that grounds for an annulment?**

Your question suggests that you or your spouse were Catholic at the time of your wedding, but that for whatever reason you chose not to have a nuptial Mass. Although canonical form for the marriages of Catholics must usually be followed (1983 CIC 1117), a nuptial Mass is not required as part of that form and hence is not required for the validity of a marriage (see 1983 CIC 1108, 1118, 1119). Therefore, the mere fact that a Mass was not celebrated at the time of your wedding would not serve as grounds for an annulment.

Question 53: **When I was growing up, my family moved frequently and, as a result, I was never in a parish long enough to get confirmed. No one asked me about this when I got married, but now I have heard that Catholics must be confirmed before getting married. Will this oversight affect my nullity petition?**

Almost certainly not. While the sacrament of Confirmation is necessary for full Christian initiation (see 1983 CIC 842 § 2, 879), it is not required for the validity of Catholic marriage. Even canon 1065 § 1, that exhorts Catholics to receive confirmation prior to getting married, only recommends reception of confirmation if it can be done "without serious inconvenience." Nowhere does canon law imply that confirmation is necessary for the validity of marriage (see 1983 CIC 10). By the way, canon 1065 § 2 goes on to recommend reception of the sacraments of penance and Holy Eucharist prior to getting married, but again as a pastoral suggestion and not as a canonical requirement. The only other way in which the failure to receive confirmation might be relevant in a nullity case would be if it were offered as evidence of "formal defection from the Church," referred to in canon 1117, that in turn might affect one's being bound by canonical form. The mere failure to receive confirmation, however, is never accepted as proof of such defection.

CHAPTER 7

QUESTIONS FROM AND ABOUT THE FORMER SPOUSE

Question 54: Will my ex be notified of my request for an annulment?

Canon law requires that every effort be made to notify, or "cite," the former spouse in a petition for nullity (1983 CIC 1507, 1620). Beyond serving legal fairness, it is usually also true that the former spouse can offer additional information about the marriage that can help the tribunal arrive at an accurate picture of the situation. The cooperation of the former spouse, therefore, is highly desirable.

However, the spouse's refusal to participate will not preclude the tribunal's hearing a petition (1983 CIC 1510, 1592). Indeed, under certain circumstances, the refusal of a respondent (or a petitioner, for that matter) to answer legitimate questions can be used as evidence in a nullity case (1983 CIC 1531 § 2).

Canon law, unlike civil law, allows tribunal judges to form reasonable conclusions about why a person might refuse to answer certain questions.

Question 55: Will my ex know what I've written or stated about our marriage?

The general rule is that both parties have the right to review all those parts of the _acts_ (basically, the documentation generated in the annulment process) that will figure in the final decision, but this answer requires some nuances. Canon 1598 § 1 protects the basic right of both parties to have an opportunity to review all the information in a case that is not already known to the parties. Other canons (see, for example, 1983 CIC 1604 § 1) forbid extra-judicial attempts to supply information to judges or otherwise to influence the outcome of cases in such a way that the other party is unaware of the attempts. But these canons, wise as they are, do not exist in a vacuum. Canon 1598 § 1, in fact, allows judges to withhold certain parts of the acts of the case from one or both parties if the judge fears that serious dangers would result from disclosing the information, provided that the right of defense remains intact. For example, a judge could ask questions that would address, without betraying, a matter withheld from disclosure.

Another aspect of informational access is important here: Not all the information presented in a case is necessary in order for the tribunal to reach a decision. One has less right to review such superfluous information. For example, in a case dealing with active drug addiction at the time of the wedding, evidence of the abuse would certainly be important to adjudication of the case, and under normal circumstances, this evidence would be made available to both parties. On the other hand, evidence about infidelity might not be relevant to the tribunal and could be withheld for serious cause from the acts of the case, provided that the judges do not use the infidelity as evidence of nullity due to factors related to drug abuse.

It is always important to remember that nullity cases are not designed to find fault or cast blame on either or both parties. Diocesan tribunals constantly resist being dragged into "he said/she said" squabbles left over from the divorce. Not relevant to the tribunal's work, for example, is whether the car that one party received in the civil divorce was a lemon or was in decent shape. Such information is frequently ignored by the tribunal. Most marriage nullity cases are adjudicated without either party asking to know what the other said.

If a request for review is made and granted, however, the inspection of the acts must be conducted within what will strike most Americans as rather stringent rules. There are too many canons to cite here, but these rules usually include having to review the acts only at the tribunal office during business hours and under the supervision of a tribunal official; not being allowed to make copies of or notes on the materials reviewed; not being allowed to discuss materials reviewed with anyone besides tribunal officers; and sometimes even not being able to review the materials personally but instead only through one's canonical advocate.

If, in the end, a party truly feels that his or her right of defense has been improperly curtailed by the tribunal's policy on the inspection of the acts, he or she can offer that as part of an appeal under canon 1628.

Question 56: **Since our divorce, I have deliberately kept my ex-husband from finding out where I live. If I file my case, will the tribunal tell him where I live?**

Tribunals gather information; they do not disperse it. There is no canonical requirement that respondents know the address of petitioners, and hence that kind of information is not typically shared. You should alert the tribunal to any special concerns you might have, though, about this kind of matter. Your former spouse's right of defense, moreover, always remains intact, and generally respondents have the right to review the evidence, no matter what its sources, that would be used to declare the marriage null (1983 CIC 1598).

Question 57: **My divorce was based in part on the extreme violence of my ex-husband. I'm very afraid of what might happen if he learns about my annulment. What can I do to protect myself from this happening?**

Bring this concern to the attention of the diocesan tribunal at (though preferably before) the time of filing your petition. Canon law is very strict about the rights of respondents to be informed of nullity proceedings and to participate in them if they wish (1983 CIC 1511). In very exceptional circumstances, there are ways to deal with the problem you have suggested. Before anything else the tribunal will have to verify your claims. Many more allegations on this point are made than are verified. Police reports, restraining orders, even medical files, can be used as evidence. In some cases tribunals are able to approach respondents about nullity petitions in a pacifying manner, explaining what is and what is not involved in the process. This might defuse problems before they arise. In very difficult cases, though, there are only two choices: First, since no one is bound to the impossible, including the morally impossible, the tribunal could decree the respondent "morally uncitable" and proceed to hear the case. Even this will not prevent the respondent from finding out about the annulment, however. For example, notification of the annulment is always sent to each party's church of baptism for entry on the baptismal register. The respondent could request a copy of that record anytime. Or if the petitioner later marries in the Church, the respondent could hear of the wedding and conclude that an annulment was declared. He or she could simply check civil marriage records for evidence of a second marriage.

Given, moreover, that marriage nullity cases, because they deal with one's status in the Church, can always be reopened by a respondent who feels that his or her rights of defense were not respected (1983 CIC 1643), there is usually little to be gained by trying to proceed without citation of a locatable respondent.

Second, if the tribunal concludes that the failure to cite the respondent really will threaten the validity of the entire proceedings, the tribunal will probably recommend withdrawal of the whole petition, at least until another time. Petitioners, in turn, have the right to appeal the refusal of the tribunal to accept a petition under those conditions (1983 CIC 1505, n. 4).

Question 58: **Since my divorce, my ex-husband has consistently been late with his child support payments. He has now filed for an annulment, because he wants to get married again. I'm willing to consider cooperating with the annulment, but only if the Church orders him to get caught up on his support payments. What are my chances of getting such an order from the tribunal?**

Next to nil. Church officials sympathize with you and with the thousands of others in similar situations. But child support payments are one of a myriad of consequences to modern divorce that canon law considers the "civil effects of marriage", and hence they fall outside the jurisdiction of the diocesan tribunal (1983 CIC 1672). Strictly speaking, by the way, the annulment does not depend on your cooperation anyway, so you cannot use the tribunal process as leverage against your husband, no matter how deserving of help you might be. That said, I would still recommend that you inform the tribunal about your problem for two reasons. First, such behavior *might* be indicative of immaturity and irresponsibility, which would be relevant to assessing your husband's matrimonial consent in the first place. Second, canon 1071 § 1, n.3 requires priests and deacons to get a local ordinary's permission prior to celebrating the marriage of one who is bound by certain obligations toward former spouses or children. By alerting the tribunal to your problem you might (again, I say, *might*) influence them toward placing a restriction—a *monitum* or *vetitum*—on your former husband's plans to remarry in the Church (1983 CIC 1077) until these matters are addressed.

Question 59: My ex-wife is long gone. How will that affect my marriage case if the tribunal can't find her?

The tribunal must make every reasonable effort to locate the respondent in a marriage case (1983 CIC 1508 § 1 and following), and your cooperation in trying to locate her will be important. The 1917 Code had several canons on acceptable methods of citation in cases involving absent or hard-to-find respondents (see 1917 CIC 1711, 1725), including the citation of family members and the posting of notices on the doors of the tribunal. The 1983 Code, however, has dropped most of those regulations and now merely states that citation must be done in accord with diocesan policies (1983 CIC 1509). Therefore, as long as citation methods respect a respondent's natural rights to notice, diocesan tribunals can and do vary among themselves as to steps to be followed in citing absent or hard-to-find respondents. Your own tribunal will advise you as to how much effort will be required in such cases.

Your concern, though, probably has to do with what happens in the event that, despite everyone's best efforts, the respondent simply cannot be located. In this case, most diocesan tribunals will issue something like a "decree of whereabouts unknown," declaring the respondent "unlocatable" and allowing the case to proceed. In such cases, the tribunal is likely to appoint an advocate for the respondent (1983 CIC 1481), although this is not strictly required. One can also expect the Defender of the Bond to consider the effects an absent respondent might have had on the case. In the end, however, a nullity case can still be heard with an unlocatable respondent, and a decision can be rendered.

Question 60: My ex-husband has gotten two letters from the tribunal, but he told me he has thrown both of them away, saying it is "my problem." Will his refusal to cooperate affect my case?

It will probably slow your case down some, but it will not, standing alone, cause it to fail. First, canon 1510 states that a respondent who refuses to accept a citation is considered to have been cited. Second, assuming the diocesan tribunal can show that the respondent was cited, canon 1592 allows the judge to declare a recalcitrant respondent absent from the proceedings and to go forward with the case. Indeed, if a legitimately cited party refuses to answer questions from the tribunal, it is up to the judges to decide what inferences can be drawn from that refusal (1983 CIC 1531 § 1). While not every refusal to answer need be construed against the party refusing, neither is it a great leap to recall that people are less inclined to answer questions when they fear that they will appear to be at fault.

It may seem obvious, yet it is worth repeating, that diocesan tribunals really do want and value the participation of respondents—they were there, they know what happened in their marriages, and in as many cases as not, they are at least as able as petitioners to provide important information to the tribunal. In any event I recommend telling the tribunal about your ex-spouse's reaction to its letters. The tribunal need not accept your word alone, but your report will be noted.

Question 61: My ex-husband suffered from mental problems all through our marriage. After our divorce he was committed to an institution. Will that pose a problem in my annulment case?

Probably not. Assuming that the diocesan tribunal can obtain jurisdiction in the case following the usual canons (1983 CIC 1673, 105 § 2), the only difference would be that your former spouse will apparently need and be accorded a "curator"—that is, one to look after his ecclesial rights (1983 CIC 1478 § 4, 1479)—and, almost certainly, a canonical advocate (1983 CIC 1481 § 1). In general, persons of diminished capacity retain all of the regular procedural rights and duties of other people, and reasonable accommodation should be offered to facilitate the exercise of those rights and duties.

Question 62: My former wife has filed for an annulment, but I want to fight it, because I know we had a valid marriage. What can I do?

First, recognize that you, the respondent, are very important in the adjudication of an annulment case and that you have numerous rights in the process. Indeed, the failure to respect your rights can result in the invalidity of the whole case (1983 CIC 1620, n. 7). Second, recognize that you are not being attacked, no matter what the circumstances of the marriage and divorce. It is your marriage that is being impugned, not you and not your former spouse. There are times when you might not feel the truth of this statement, especially if grounds are joined on your possible canonical incapacity for marriage, your possible failure to consent adequately to marriage as the Church understands and proclaims it, or your possible failure to observe canonical form if it was required. Third, participate in the case. Respond truthfully and completely when the tribunal asks for information, and know in advance that most diocesan tribunals will try to be more accommodating of respondents' concerns and schedules than they are of petitioners.' Why? Well, if for no better reason, tribunals know that petitioners want something from them, and hence petitioners are likely to be more flexible in working with tribunals; respondents, on the other hand, often do not want anything from tribunals (except fair treatment), but respondents' cooperation can greatly facilitate what tribunals need to do, namely, reach accurate decisions. Besides, mistakes made in the treatment of respondents are more likely to cast doubt on the canonical force of tribunals decisions than are mistakes made in the treatment of petitioners.

On the other hand, do not mistakenly conclude that if the respondent's contribution is so important in an annulment case, the withholding of that cooperation will only hurt the petitioner's chances of getting the annulment. Wrong. It is quite possible, and it often happens, that more than enough evidence of canonical nullity is adduced even without a respondent's cooperation. Indeed, a respondent's (or, for that matter, a petitioner's) failure to cooperate in a case can be used as evidence against his or her case (1983 CIC 1531 § 2). There is no such thing as the Fifth Amendment in canon law.

There are, of course, many other ways to oppose an annulment. To take just one example, if the tribunal asks you to name witnesses who can testify in support of your position, name them. And if the tribunal does not ask you for witnesses (which would be unusual, though not technically illegal under canon 1553), propose them anyway. Make sure the tribunal knows that you are serious about wanting your side of the story heard.

In the end, though, all of these other ways of opposing an annulment are better explained in concrete cases by your own canonical advocate. Respondents (as well as petitioners) have the right to use a qualified canonical advocate (1983 CIC 1481 § 1) and diocesan tribunals are encouraged to keep advocates available for parties in marriage nullity cases (1983 CIC 1490). It is not precisely determined in canon law just when the right to a canon lawyer becomes operative (although it is certainly no later than the "joinder of issues" discussed in canons 1513 and 1516, which is still early enough to be effective in most cases). An actual request for a canon lawyer made at almost any stage of the proceedings is likely to be honored by the tribunal for all of the reasons suggested above.

Remember, finally, that every canonical case is designed to identify the truth of the matter, not to grant victory to one or the other party. If you are committed to finding the truth of the situation in accord with canon law and no matter what the outcome, your participation in an annulment case is much more likely to contribute to an accurate decision by the tribunal.

Question 63: I don't trust American tribunals. Can I request that my ex-spouse's annulment case be heard by the tribunal in Rome?

You can request it, but that does not necessarily mean your request is going to be honored. If you have already been cited by the diocesan tribunal, that tribunal is allowed to continue processing the case unless and until informed otherwise by Rome (1983 CIC 1417 § 2, 1512, n. 2). The summoning of a case to Rome is rare, but it might be ordered if, for example, serious malfeasance with irreparable harm were being plausibly asserted against the local tribunal. As is true of most legal systems, higher canonical courts tend not to interfere in the operation of lower courts, since so many early fears of litigants prove to be unwarranted when their case is actually heard. Besides, the right of appeal for all parties is protected by canon law (1983 CIC 1628), so there is time for higher tribunals, including those of Rome, to get involved if necessary.

If you have not yet actually been cited by the local tribunal, your chances of having your case heard in Rome are somewhat better (1983 CIC 1417 § 1, 1444), but still unlikely.

Question 64: **A few months back, I received a letter from my local diocese asking if I had any objections to a diocese in another state hearing my ex-wife's annulment case. I wrote back saying I was opposed to an annulment in any diocese. Now I get a letter from the other tribunal telling me they are hearing her case and asking if I would like to participate. Don't these people get the message? I don't want an annulment, period. How can I stop this from proceeding?**

You cannot block your ex-wife's petition. Both dioceses probably understood your message very clearly. My guess is that you did not understand *their* questions. You were not being asked whether you wanted an annulment, whether you would agree to one, or whether you would consent to or cooperate in the process. You were merely asked, I am sure, whether you had any objections to the out-of-state diocese's hearing your former spouse's case, in accord with canon 1673, n. 3. That's all. You wrote back and expressed your opposition to any annulment, anywhere, anytime, which you are free to do—a response that will doubtless be noted. But you did not say anything that suggested a reasonable basis for the judicial vicar of your diocese to reject the lawful request of the other diocese to hear your former spouse's petition. Apparently, that permission was thereafter granted, and the other diocese is proceeding with the case. Note, even if you had said something that looked like a plausible basis for rejecting the request, your judicial vicar would not have necessarily been bound to uphold your objection, although your chances would have been better.

In any case, the out-of-state diocesan tribunal is, almost certainly, proceeding correctly in accord with canon law. That is why you are now being asked by it to participate in the case, even though your opposition to the annulment remains as strong as ever. Remember, canon law favors the upholding of marriages (1983 CIC 1060, 1526, 1608 § 4). Your marriage cannot be declared null unless it can be proven to have been null from the beginning. The case will be heard without you if necessary (1983 CIC 1592, 1593), but it would be much better for all concerned to have your input.

Question 65: **I just got the shock of my life. I got a letter from the Church telling me my marriage of over twenty years, which ended in divorce a few years ago, has been annulled. This is the very first I have heard about this. Why wasn't I asked to be involved? What can I do about this?**

What you have described is extremely rare, but it can happen. Canon law insists that great efforts be made to include respondents in nullity cases and that ample measures be taken to protect their rights even if they are absent from the proceedings (1983 CIC 1511 & 1592–1593). Whatever tribunal(s) heard your case, they would have kept records of the efforts made to contact you. It is possible, though, that a mistake (or even fraud) kept you from being notified in a timely manner. What to do now depends somewhat on what exactly you were told in your letter, that is, it depends somewhat on just where in the total canonical process your case is. Contact the tribunal that wrote to you and tell them what you told me. Stay calm in doing it, because diocesan tribunals not infrequently get complaints like yours from people who in fact knew what was going on all along, but who did not take things seriously until they got a letter telling them the annulment had been declared. You will probably be asked to help the tribunal identify just how it was that you did not receive canonical notice until so late in the process. Considering that diocesan tribunals feel as badly as people like you do in cases like this (not to mention that such a scenario raises doubts about the validity of the decision under canon 1620, n.7), they will probably bend over backward to set things right. If, however, at any point you do not feel that you are being treated fairly or honestly by the tribunal, contact independent canonical counsel for guidance and help.

CHAPTER 8

QUESTIONS FROM AND ABOUT
WITNESSES IN AN ANNULMENT CASE

Question 66: **Will I be allowed to name witnesses in my marriage case?**

Yes. In almost all cases both the petitioner and the respondent are asked to name witnesses, although the mere fact that one or even both parties have named a particular witness does not mean that the tribunal must hear that witness (1983 CIC 1547). Moreover, the tribunal can call witnesses of its own choosing, but except in cases requiring expert testimony (1983 CIC 1574, 1575), this is not usually done. Respondents tend to be somewhat less likely than petitioners to name witnesses.

Question 67: **What kinds of questions am I, or my witnesses, likely to be asked if I file my marriage case?**

Because nullity cases are mostly concerned with the conditions and circumstances of the parties at and before the time of the wedding, most of the questions will be designed to illuminate that period of time for the tribunal. That is not to say, however, that there will be no questions about the actual progress and demise of the marriage, for there certainly will be. Questions tend to be open-ended, inviting longer rather than shorter responses. As a practical matter, and unlike civil courts, the parties and witnesses in canonical nullity cases are usually encouraged to offer whatever information they think useful, instead of narrowly limiting themselves to direct responses to carefully crafted questions. Indeed, "yes and no" answers to tribunal questions are rarely helpful. No area of personal life is out of bounds for questions, if that is what you are wondering about. While tribunals have no prurient desire to delve into private (including sexual) matters, they will inquire about them if such matters are relevant to the issues posed in a case. For the most part, questions posed to witnesses generally track those posed to the parties. Sometimes, of course, parties and witnesses are asked to respond to additional, more specific questions that might have occurred as a result of the "instruction," or investigation, of the case (1983 CIC 1570).

Witnesses are usually asked to swear or affirm the truthfulness of their answers (1983 CIC 1562). The canonical preference is that witnesses be interviewed at the tribunal office (1983 CIC 1558 § 1) but this is often impractical and not necessary in order to obtain reliable testimony. Generally, witnesses are interviewed alone, and only in exceptional circumstances are other persons (such as the Defender of the Bond) present for the interview (1983 CIC 1560, 1561).

Question 68: **What kinds of people make good witnesses?**

The best witnesses in marriage nullity cases are knowledgeable, honest, and articulate. It does little good to name as a witness someone who, for example, knew you or your former spouse for only a few months toward the end of your marriage. At the risk of oversimplifying, the tribunal is not concerned about how your marriage ended but rather with how it started. Witnesses should be able to speak about you or your former spouse prior to and at the time of the wedding. Thus considered, parents generally make pretty good witnesses. In my experience, mothers are more likely to give useful overviews of one or both spouses' youth and courtship, whereas fathers tend to answer only the more direct questions. So be it: Most tribunals recommend the naming of both parents (including step-parents) as witnesses. Siblings make excellent witnesses, because their experiences often closely track those of the parties. Siblings also seem to be less likely to "interpret" their testimony than are some parents (who might feel that their performance in raising their children is being indirectly questioned by a nullity case). Most tribunals encourage and readily accept sibling testimony.

Best men and maids of honor are often named as witnesses, but somehow they tend not to be as useful as one might think. The friends of youth see only with the eyes of youth, and in a mobile society such as ours, these early friends often lose touch with the parties. Still the tribunal might well ask for them, so listing them will save time in most cases. Other friends from that period of time can be named as well, of course.

Recommending that witnesses be honest is not meant to imply that witnesses might lie to Church tribunals, although they do every day. Rather, the suggestion is that people who are less likely to shade their testimony, as well as people whose general lifestyle shows maturity and integrity, be named as witnesses. For example, in a case turning on questions of pre-wedding drug or alcohol abuse, the naming of former but unreformed drug buddies might not accomplish much, for such witnesses are often motivated to minimize their, and the party's, drug or alcohol involvement. On the other hand, reformed alcoholics tend to be very honest and accurate about levels of substance abuse. What the tribunal needs are honest, accurate reports.

Finally, witnesses who are likely to be articulate should be named. This quality is, in some cases, hard to predict, but it should be considered. Many petitions stall, or even fail, because the witnesses offer only a short series of "yes and no" answers to questions requiring much more careful thought. You should know that most tribunals will accommodate witnesses' requests to be interviewed rather than filling out questionnaires. They also will allow them to respond in writing if travel to the tribunal offices is difficult.

Similarly, tribunals are to make special efforts to accommodate witnesses whose first language is not English (1983 CIC 1471).

If, during the investigation of your case, problems develop because of the poor quality of witness testimony, you will probably be contacted and asked to name additional witnesses. Such requests are often a sign that the case is stalling and might well be the last attempt a tribunal will make to move the case toward resolution.

Of course, if the testimony that comes in is canonically reliable but points to the validity of the marriage, so be it. The tribunal is dedicated to the truth of the situation, not to saying yes to every nullity petition it gets. You can only do the best you can do.

You name the best witnesses you can find, and then you let the tribunal process take its course.

Question 69: **Will my children be called as witnesses if I file a nullity petition?**

Strictly speaking, anyone above the age of fourteen is considered eligible to testify before a diocesan tribunal, and in some cases children even younger than that could be called (1983 CIC 1550). But most tribunals avoid calling children as witnesses in the marriage nullity cases of their parents for several reasons. First, marriage nullity cases are concerned primarily with facts and circumstances prior to and at the time of the wedding. In most cases children could not testify because they were not around at the times most relevant to the tribunal's inquiry. This is changing as more cases of divorce in "blended" families, with older children present during and before the impugned marriage, come before diocesan tribunals for adjudication. A second obstacle to calling children as witnesses lies in the fact that either party can request the exclusion of a witness based on "just cause" (1983 CIC 1555). One party or the other might well offer just cause as to why children should not be called as witnesses in the nullity cases of their parents. A tribunal would be hard pressed not to honor such a request by either or both parties, although, strictly speaking, it is not bound to do so. Moreover, judges are to limit excessive numbers of witnesses (1983 CIC 1553), and a judge may decide that child witnesses are "excessive" in a particular case.

In brief, the calling of children (especially younger children) as witnesses in a marriage case is rare but not impossible. If you are still concerned about this, speak to your advocate or the tribunal as soon as possible.

Question 70: **Will I be allowed to name my therapist as a witness in my annulment case?**

You may list your therapist as a witness, but it will be up to the tribunal to decide whether the therapist will be contacted (1983 CIC 1547, 1575, 1581). You should expect to pay any fees your therapist might charge for testifying. Several factors will influence the tribunal's decision on calling an expert you suggest, and the type of therapist you list will make a difference in whether he or she is called as a witness. For example, a psychiatrist will more likely be able to give the tribunal the kind of technical information it needs in adjudicating a marriage case than will a social worker. Similarly, therapists with special certification in marriage and family life will be more helpful than therapists who specialize in occupational adjustment disorders. On the other hand, therapists with special training in the areas of most concern to the tribunal in a given case (for example, drug and alcohol counselors in a case involving substance abuse) will more likely be called as witnesses than will even a marriage and family life counselor.

A therapist with a long record of involvement with one or both parties will more likely be called upon than will a therapist who knew one or both parties only briefly (typically, after the divorce, which is the least useful period for evidence gathering). Therapists who make use of standard personality profiles and psychological/psychiatric batteries tend to be more useful to the tribunal than are therapists who do not, or cannot, administer and interpret such tests. Those who have worked with diocesan tribunals in the past are more likely to be called than are those who know little or nothing about the issues with which tribunals must be concerned. This is usually a matter of efficiency.

It is not necessary that the therapist be Catholic in order to testify. Not all therapists are Catholic, of course, and not all Catholic therapists share the Church's commitment to marriage. As a tribunal judge, however, I have seen therapist reports that, deliberately or otherwise, argued about Church teaching on marriage rather than focusing on the facts of the case before them. This does no one any good.

From time to time the tribunal itself will seek the opinion of a psychological or psychiatric expert (or other kind of expert for that matter) to help it understand the facts of a particular case. Strictly speaking, if an expert is engaged by the tribunal only to examine the evidence already presented in a case, and the party or parties are not going to be charged an additional fee for such review, the tribunal can submit the materials for the expert's review without notifying the parties in advance. This is done only rarely, however, and in any event, the parties are free to make replies to the opinions of experts (1983 CIC 1598 and following).

Alternatively, the tribunal might suggest that one (or both) parties in a nullity case undergo an evaluation with a counselor approved by the diocesan tribunal, and the counselor will then make his or her report directly to the tribunal. In these cases, the party or parties undergoing the evaluation are almost always required to pay any associated fees (1983 CIC 1580), and frequently the results of the evaluation are not shared with the parties afterward. This is because the expert is not attempting to serve the parties but rather to assist the tribunal. If such an option is going to be suggested in your case, you will be notified in advance and your permission will be requested. Your consent cannot be forced by the tribunal; you are free to say no. Occasionally, however, your refusal will mean that insufficient evidence of nullity is adduced in your petition and your petition will fail.

One should be aware that civil laws on confidentiality might prevent a therapist from answering diocesan tribunal questions regarding one spouse without the consent of the other spouse. Such additional consent is not always provided, of course, and there is little the tribunal can do to encourage it. Still, most therapists are able to answer questions about one spouse. Finally, be aware that therapists differ in the length of time they retain client records. I have seen important questions posed to therapists, with consent to answer provided, only to have the therapist reply that the client's records are no longer available.

Question 71: **I've been talking with a priest for many years about the problems in my marriage. Can I ask him to serve as a witness in my nullity petition?**

That depends. If you have gone to confession to this priest and you would now like him to testify about things you brought to the confessional (perhaps as evidence that the factors that you claim eventually destroyed the marriage were present from the very beginning), the answer is no (1983 CIC 1550 § 2, n. 2, 983, 1388). This applies even if you specifically authorize the priest to relate what he heard in your confession. The Church simply will not allow anything that could even appear to jeopardize the seal of confession. Alternatively, even if you went to confession to this priest, you might want him to relate things that you discussed outside of confession. Strictly speaking, the priest is canonically free to relate such information with your consent, but be aware that you are putting him in a very delicate position. In any event, it is fully within the authority of the tribunal to reject such a priest as a witness, even over your objections. If the priest so much as hints that he feels the sacramental seal to be an issue in his testimony, you had better expect him to be stricken from the witness list (see also canon 1548 2, n. 1, that allows clerics to avoid testifying, if they wish, on anything made known to them in connection with sacred ministry).

Finally, it is possible that there is no question of the seal of confession or ministerial confidentiality being threatened if your priest advisor testifies. In such cases you are free to name the priest as a witness, and the tribunal can exercise its normal discretion in calling or not calling the priest. Personally, however, I find parish priests to be rather weak as witnesses in marriage nullity cases. Most of their information tends to come from just one spouse in a troubled marriage, their contact with troubled couples usually does not significantly predate the wedding, and they are generally so busy with other things that what they know and say tends to be, from a canonical point of view at least, rather superficial. Occasionally, of course, a priest witness overcomes all of these shortcomings, and he serves the tribunal's needs well.

Question 72: **I can't think of any witnesses for my marriage case. What can I do?**

This is a serious problem, and it could result in the failure of your petition. But it is not the virtually insurmountable problem it used to be.

Because marriage nullity cases are, understandably, considered to deal with the public good (1983 CIC 1691), certain special rules apply to them. One of these says that, standing alone, the mere declaration of a party cannot be accepted as full proof on a point (1983 CIC 1536 § 2). While tribunal judges can work with a party to try to adduce additional evidence (1983 CIC 1530, 1452 § 2), at least some other corroboration of the petitioner's claim will have to be forthcoming before a tribunal can even think about reaching moral certitude of nullity (see 1983 CIC 1060, 1608 § 4).

For that matter, in most cases, the testimony of a single witness (as distinguished from a party) on any given point is also usually not considered full proof of that point (1983 CIC 1573). But here is where the 1983 Code is somewhat more lenient in its norms on the interpretation of evidence than was the 1917 Code. Canon 1573 of the 1983 Code, for example, does allow the testimony of a single witness to carry a point if, fairly considered, the general circumstances suggest such testimony to be credible. It is up to the judges to assess those circumstances (1983 CIC 1572).

Moreover, even if the only evidence on a point comes from the declaration of the petitioner or respondent, the 1983 Code allows such declarations to carry some weight if they amount to what canon law considers a "judicial confession" against the party himself or herself (1983 CIC 1535, 1536). People tend not to want to admit faults or flaws in themselves, so canon law is willing to give some higher credence to statements made by a party that reflect poorly on that party. On the other hand, tribunal judges, to say nothing of Defenders of the Bond, will understandably look carefully at petitioner or respondent declarations that suddenly and conveniently are filled with admissions that, however poorly they reflect on the party making them, also make it more likely that the annulment petition will be granted. The Church is all in favor of growth in self-knowledge and the free admission of personal faults and flaws; it just wants those admissions to be accurate.

The tribunal will usually work with the parties to help them uncover witnesses, but it will not do the parties' work for them. In a marriage case the burden of proof is on the petitioner (1983 CIC 1526). While going into a marriage case with few or no witnesses is not the nearly insurmountable obstacle it used to be, doing so makes it less likely that the tribunal will be able to reach moral certitude of nullity.

Question 73: **Last year a couple with whom my husband and I have been friends for many years got divorced. My husband and I were named as witnesses in a nullity case filed by one of them. We very much want to avoid taking sides in this tragic affair. On the other hand, we want to cooperate with the Church, if we really ought to. Please advise.**

Your concern is a common one, but it usually grows out of a misunderstanding of how canon law in general, and marriage nullity cases in particular, are conducted. Although both parties in a canonical nullity case can name witnesses, it is up to the tribunal to decide which witnesses are actually called (1983 CIC 1547). You have been notified, therefore, not so much that one side or the other wants your help in arguing their case but that the diocesan tribunal wants your help in making an informed decision.

Whether your testimony is taken in person or in writing, and regardless of who requested that you be called as a witness, you will quickly see that the tribunal's questions are not geared to helping or hurting one side or the other in a marriage case. Rather, you are being asked to describe as objectively as possible the actual facts and circumstances of the marriage. If, in fact, this reflects better or worse on one of the parties, so be it. It often happens that witnesses suggested by one party end up giving testimony about that party that is unflattering. Again, that is normal and acceptable. In any event, as a witness you are not being asked to take sides or to determine whether either or both parties "deserve" an annulment. You are being asked, by the tribunal, for information that the tribunal needs to make an accurate decision.

If, however, you are still concerned that your participation in a case might hurt you or someone you love or that your relationship with either or both parties might suffer (and you have already taken into consideration that your failure to participate might do the very same thing), there are two options open to you.

First, you can ask that your testimony be held confidential from the parties. Tribunal judges have the authority to withhold some testimony from the parties under canon 1598, but such authority is to be used only in serious cases. Hurt feelings are usually not considered a sufficient basis upon which to withhold information from the parties.

Second, you could invoke canon 1548 § 2, n. 2 to avoid testifying in a case. This canon allows persons who fear that ill-repute, dangerous problems, or other evils will be imposed on them or their loved ones in the event that they testify.

But let us be frank here: Whatever the legitimate authority of a diocesan tribunal to seek testimony from a witness (1983 CIC 1557), it has next to no power to enforce that request. The Church does not have police to arrest defiant witnesses, nor does it have jails to put them in. If a witness really refuses to cooperate, even for unjust reasons, there is not much the tribunal can do about it. That said, I only repeat that "fear of testifying" is often exaggerated by potential witnesses.

CHAPTER 9

THE EFFECTS OF AN ANNULMENT

Question 74: **If one spouse gets an annulment, does it count for the other spouse as well?**

Yes. An annulment is an official declaration that what appeared to be a marriage was in fact not one. Just as it takes two people to make a marriage, so an annulment means that neither of the two persons were truly married, even if the canonical reasons for nullity were centered on just one of the two spouses.

Question 75: **Will an annulment decide who was to blame for our divorce?**

No. The annulment process is neither designed nor intended to attribute blame or fault to one side or the other. Remember that the annulment process is the Church's way of determining as accurately as possible whether the parties in an impugned marriage were validly married in the first place. The technical issues in annulment cases are the purely canonical ones of capacity, consent, and form. This does not mean, however, that one party cannot be the focus of tribunal investigation more than the other. If grounds for nullity are more obvious, or are more easily proven, with one party than the other (indeed, perhaps the other party exhibited no grounds for nullity), then that party will be the one upon whom the case is heard. Even then, fault is simply not a factor in the tribunal's treatment of the case. That said, many people experience in the annulment process an opportunity to reflect on an important and usually stressful period in their lives. In doing so, they often come to learn more about their own strengths and weaknesses. This growth in self-knowledge can help in the divorce healing process, and in some cases it can improve prospects for a successful future marriage in the Church.

Question 76: Will an annulment render the children illegitimate?

No. But this answer requires some explanation. First, let us say a few words on the notion of illegitimacy. It stinks. Babies are not illegitimate, no matter how illegitimate might have been the situation in which they were conceived. Regardless of whether their parents were married at the time of conception, babies are conceived in the image and likeness of God. Second, illegitimacy no longer carries any significant canonical consequences. For example, children born illegitimate are no longer hampered in seeking ordination as they were under the 1917 Code (see 1917 CIC 984, n. 1, as compared to 1983 CIC 1041). The only reason the concept of legitimacy is still treated in the 1983 Code at all is because some nations, by treaty with the Holy See, will accept canonical declarations of nullity as civil divorces, and that raises the possibility that post-divorce civil questions of child support and inheritance could be clouded if legitimacy were not treated in canon law. These kinds of concerns, however, are not relevant in the United States. Notwithstanding all these reasons to remove worry about canonical legitimacy, questions are still frequently raised about the effects of annulments on the legitimacy of children. Canon 1137 states that children born or conceived of a valid or *putative* marriage are considered legitimate. Canon 1061 § 3 calls *putative* those marriages that, although invalid, are nevertheless celebrated in good faith by at least one of the parties, until that time, if any, when both parties become certain of its nullity. The great majority of the formal nullity cases coming before diocesan tribunals in fact involve at least one, usually two, persons who enter marriage in good faith, hence entering at least a putative marriage, resulting in the legitimacy of the children. But there are a few exceptions to this general conclusion.

If a child is born less than one hundred days after the canonical wedding (not the civil ceremony, if there was one), he or she is not canonically presumed to be legitimate (1983 CIC 1138 § 2). Thus, the rushed religious wedding some people feel is necessary before the baby is born does not always result in the canonical legitimation of the child. Notice, however, that legitimacy arises from the timing of the wedding relative to the birth of the baby; it has nothing to do with the later annulment. Frankly, though, it should be admitted that canon law is behind the scientific curve here: It is not uncommon today for children to be born very immaturely and survive. Such children fall in between a canonical crack, even if they are legitimately conceived.

On the other hand, if a child is born to parents not married or only civilly married, but then the parents later validly, or even putatively, marry, such marriage automatically renders the child or children canonically legitimate (1983 CIC 1139). Even here, though, the later annulment of the marriage does not render the children canonically illegitimate. Finally, canon 1139 states that children can be legitimated by *rescript* of the Holy See.

In brief, the granting of an annulment petition does nothing to affect the legitimacy of children. That status, to the scant degree it has any canonical significance, is determined prior to the time any question of annulment is raised.

Question 77: **I have been told that even if my annulment goes through, there is still a very good chance that I would still not be allowed to remarry in the Church. What is this all about? Who gives them that right?**

An annulment only determines that what was believed to be a valid marriage was not one as far as the Church is concerned. In reaching that conclusion, the Church states that the parties whom it earlier presumed to be bound by a marriage are not actually bound, and hence, in that respect, and in that respect only, they are free to enter marriage in the Church (see 1983 CIC 1085 § 1). But it often happens that, in adjudicating a marriage case, the tribunal finds a condition that not only seriously affected one's capacity or consent at the time of the wedding but is clearly still at work in either (or both) of the parties. For example, if the active alcoholism that destroyed one's capacity or consent for marriage the first time around remains unaddressed, there is little reason to doubt its deleterious effects on marriage the second time around as well. No one wants to see that happen, so using canon 1077 § 1, the tribunal can impose a *vetitum* on the affected party (or parties). A *vetitum* is a prohibition against a future marriage until, in this example, the alcoholism is competently addressed. Sounds good so far, but this is where the problems start.

First, the *vetitum* can last only as long as the problem lasts. This, too, sounds reasonable, until one realizes that many of the factors that destroy matrimonial capacity or consent do not fit into neat time-bound patterns whose resolutions can be accurately spotted. Moreover, the canonical presumptions in favor of matrimonial capacity and consent (1983 CIC 1058, 1101) keep pressure on Church officials to lift prohibitions sooner rather than later.

Second, a *vetitum* can affect only current subjects of the bishop whose tribunal issued it. Of course, people move from place to place over time, and while neighboring dioceses try to be respectful of each other's *vetita,* there is no strict requirement that they do so. As the years and miles accumulate, the perception of the first tribunal might not be shared by the second. Furthermore, the tribunal that hears the nullity case might have jurisdiction over the respondent only for the purpose of hearing the marriage case (1983 CIC 1673, nn. 1, 3, or 4), leaving little apparent basis for canon 1077 to apply.

Third, and most important, although marrying under an unresolved *vetitum* is illicit, no prohibition by a bishop or tribunal can, by itself, prevent the *putative validity* of such a marriage. At least three canons (1983 CIC 1075, 1076, and 1077) make it quite clear that only the pope can prohibit a given marriage upon pain of invalidity. There are, unfortunately, some cases of couples who, even with the cooperation of Catholic ministers, enter marriage in violation of their prohibitions. Such scenarios, even if not automatically null, are tailor-made for disaster.

Clearly, canons 1075 and 1077 reflect a concern that marriage, and the faithful's right to enter marriage, could suffer abuse (deliberate or otherwise) if the bishops or their tribunals could use *vetita* as grounds for annulments. On the other hand, having to stand by and watch people serially enter invalid marriages does not seem to serve the common good either.

Ideally, people who receive a *vetitum* during an annulment process (and they are not commonly imposed) will recognize that such a prohibition represents the dispassionate conclusion of experienced observers who only want to help. (I am sorry if that sounds quaint, but it is true.) Meanwhile, family and friends can help by not greeting the news of an upcoming second wedding as if it were going to be an automatic cure-all for whatever went wrong the first time. It is difficult not to feel joy at a wedding announcement. But these days, a little prudent reserve might be helpful too.

Question 78: **My annulment has been approved, and I just got a letter from the tribunal saying the appellate court agreed with my annulment. But the letter also said that I have a** *monitum* **on me and that I will have to contact the tribunal before making any marriage plans in the future. Please explain what this is all about.**

I assume that when you say a *monitum*, you do not mean a *vetitum*. A *vetitum*, for reasons given elsewhere, is frankly a more serious matter than is a *monitum*. But having said that, I do not wish to understate the importance of what you have been told. A *monitum* is not an official canonical institution, at least not in marriage nullity cases. Literally "a warning," notice of a *monitum* by a tribunal is just the tribunal's way of saying, in effect, "Your annulment has been declared, but we are concerned lest you rush into another marriage before taking some time to digest what has happened and to prepare better for a successful marriage." Assuming that you and the tribunal are using the terms correctly, a *monitum* is not a prohibition against a future marriage in the Church, as would be the case with a *vetitum*. Rather, a *monitum* is a friendly, if firm, suggestion by knowledgeable people that some issues raised by your first marriage and divorce should be considered, perhaps with professional help, before you enter another marriage. The tribunal will explain its precise concerns if and when you contact it.

CHAPTER 10

IF THE ANSWER IS NO

Question 79: **After four years of what I thought was a happy marriage, my ex-husband took some drugs on a bet and, within a year, he was completely addicted, unemployed, violent, and we were bankrupt. We were divorced and I applied for an annulment, which was denied! There is absolutely no way I'm going back to him. What does the Catholic Church expect me to do?**

When you say your nullity petition was denied, I assume you mean you received a formal negative decision, not merely an opinion, from a diocesan tribunal. I assume that your case was heard, that you have no reasonable basis for appeal, and that you have discussed all of this with a canonical advisor of your choosing.

That said, I am not entirely surprised by what seems to be the outcome of your case, since your description in the broadest terms paints a picture of a good marriage gone tragically bad. Marriages that die are not necessarily null; that is a fact of canon law, derived from Church teaching, in turn resting in the Truth that is Christ. Only marriages that were null from the beginning can be declared null in the end.

Now to your question about what the Church expects of you. Well, I can say that it does not expect you to go back to your former spouse, although strictly speaking you are free to do that if circumstances warrant it. Generally, validly married couples have a right and duty "to preserve the conjugal life" (1983 CIC 1135, 1151), but no one is bound to an impossible or dangerous marriage situation (1983 CIC 1153).

Incredible as it might seem, marriages worse than the one you describe have come back together, albeit with grace and hard work—not many, maybe, but some. Christ makes all things new. I am not going to gloss over damage that such conduct works on a marriage or minimize the efforts that it can, and probably would, require to put things aright. But marriage is a sacrament for baptized couples, and every sacrament is a source of strength and renewal in Christ for its recipients.

In any event, the Church does not expect anything in particular from you based on the fact of your divorce that it does not already expect of you based on your baptism and your call to holiness, that remains despite your divorce. The Church does, however, expect you not to do one thing: Namely, it expects you not to attempt another marriage in the Church, since for as long as nullity cannot be proven and your former spouse is alive, you are considered bound by the marriage you entered and that someone else betrayed.

Question 80: I've been told that my annulment petition will probably not be approved, but that I could apply for a Pauline Privilege. What is that and why do I qualify?

The Pauline Privilege, so named because it derives from St. Paul's writings in 1 Corinthians 7:12-15, is treated in canons 1143 and following. Basically, the tribunal is telling you that, based on a preliminary assessment of the facts of your case, you might be able to contract a new, valid marriage even if your first marriage cannot be proven null. I will assume your case fits the most common type of case in which the Pauline Privilege is possible. Variations between what follows and what is actually true in your case, however, will not automatically mean that your chances of using the Pauline Privilege are gone. Nor does meeting each requirement guarantee your eligibility for the Pauline Privilege. This is only a basic guide:

1) Neither you nor your former spouse were baptized at the time of your wedding. This has to be canonically proven.

2) You received Christian (but not necessarily Catholic) baptism after your wedding, and your former spouse has not. This also must be canonically proven.

3) Your unbaptized former spouse canonically "departed." Usually this means that he or she sought a divorce for almost any reason, but strictly speaking, separation or divorce is not canonically required.

Even if you filed for the civil divorce (which is permissible), you must not be improperly the cause of the breakup. For example, you must not have committed adultery against your former spouse. It must somehow, fairly considered, be your former spouse who will not let you live your new Christian faith. You need not use the Pauline Privilege immediately upon your baptism, and continued cohabitation, including sexual relations, can be shared after your baptism without prejudice to the operation of the Pauline Privilege.

4) Following a canonical investigation and verification of the above points (all of which can be conducted by local Church officials), you would be permitted to contract a new marriage with a Catholic, with a non-Catholic Christian, or even with an unbaptized person. The new marriage, not your baptism, would *dissolve*, not annul, your first marriage.

By the way, being told (presumably by tribunal officials) that your original nullity petition "probably will not be approved" is not the same thing as getting a formal decision from them, although it might well be an informed prediction. Keep in mind that you have the right to a decision on the merits of your petition, if you decide to exercise those rights. Finally, you need not exhaust the Pauline Privilege option before filing for an annulment nor be rejected in an annulment proceeding before applying for the Pauline Privilege.

Because the amount of tribunal work necessary in a Pauline Privilege case is almost the same as the amount of work required in a formal nullity case, most tribunals will ask for roughly the same fee for either case. If you have questions about this, just ask.

Question 81: If my annulment is not granted by my diocesan tribunal, can I take my case to another tribunal?

Probably, but be careful here. If your nullity petition was actually heard but received a negative sentence (that is, if the diocesan tribunal officially said no to your request), you have the right to appeal that negative decision to the next higher court (1983 CIC 1628). However, once a diocesan tribunal establishes jurisdiction over a case, it more or less keeps it, so you have to deal with the consequences of that negative sentence. Therefore, even if you were to file your case anew in another tribunal, mentioning nothing about your negative sentence from the first tribunal, the second tribunal would probably be acting invalidly, albeit unwittingly, if it accepted the case (1983 CIC 1415, 1512, n. 2). Do not try to deceive a diocesan tribunal about issues related to its jurisdiction. Marriage nullity cases, because they deal with the status of persons in the Church, are canonically easy to reopen, even without your consent (1983 CIC 1430, 1643, 1674). Any hint of deception on these kinds of points could bring a swift tribunal response.

On the other hand, if your case was not formally heard by the diocesan tribunal, but for various reasons it does not appear that your petition can be granted, you could ask for the transfer of your case to another competent tribunal. You might be asked to withdraw formally your case from the first tribunal (1983 CIC 1524), but as long as you fully disclose the fact of the earlier filing and why you wish a new tribunal to hear your case, the second tribunal will give it a fair consideration. This is not "forum shopping," as the concept is understood in civil law, and if it were, canon law itself would probably prevent you from doing it (see, for example, 1983 CIC 1488 § 2). Transfer of cases is not a common practice, but reasons for which it might be considered (not necessarily granted, however) would include excessive backlog at the first tribunal or the relocation of either or both parties in the case to another diocese.

Question 82: If my annulment does not go through, will I be prohibited from receiving the sacraments?

If you are prohibited from receiving the sacraments, it is because your marital status is already irregular, not because your annulment was not declared. If, for example, you are divorced but have not since then attempted marriage outside the Church, your right to approach the sacraments is not affected at all. A second marriage, however, would raise a question about your participation in the sacraments.

Divorce and remarriage outside the Church generally places one in objectively grave sin and therefore prevents one from receiving the Eucharist (1983 CIC 915). For those who might doubt my interpretation of this canon on technical grounds, I would call attention to the Congregation for the Doctrine of the Faith *Letter on the Reception of Communion by Divorced and Remarried Catholics* (September 14, 1994, paragraph 9) upholding this same view, which is the traditional understanding.

You can, of course, approach the sacrament of Penance at any time, if you have firm purpose of amendment (1983 CIC 980). This would imply, however, if not a separation from your new spouse (that might be impractical for any number of reasons), at least a resolution not to engage in conjugal relations reserved only for married couples. You may also receive the sacrament of Anointing of the Sick under basically the same conditions (1983 CIC 1007)

CHAPTER 11

Miscellaneous Questions

Question 83: **If a Catholic gets married in the Church, but then gets divorced and marries someone else civilly without an annulment, is he or she excommunicated?**

Not since October 22, 1977, when Pope Paul VI authorized dropping the American ecclesiastical legislation (dating from the Council of Baltimore in 1884) which had imposed excommunication on Catholics who remarry outside the Church. And, if there is anyone out there who divorced and remarried before 1977, they should know that the same removal of penalties applies to them as well (1983 CIC 1313 ,6 2). Remarriage outside the Church, however, is still objectively gravely sinful and does affect one's ability to participate in the sacraments, including the Eucharist.

Question 84: **What is an internal forum solution? It has been suggested as a possible way to work through my marriage situation.**

In the marriage and divorce context, the internal forum solution is presented by some as a way of allowing divorced and remarried Catholics to approach the sacraments without first canonically resolving their irregular marital status in the Church. Basically, the theory holds that those who cannot canonically prove the invalidity of a former marriage, sincerely believed to be invalid, should not be deprived of the sacraments after remarrying since it is not their fault that canon law does not recognize the invalidity of that earlier marriage. Depending on who is presenting the solution, it might or might not require consultation with a priest before implementation; it might or might not require receiving sacraments at a parish where one is not known; and it even might or might not require having filed a marriage case with the diocesan tribunal, let alone having exhausted the opportunities for appeal. Regardless of how such variations on the theme are answered, and regardless of who is presenting the solution for consideration, the internal forum solution is *not* a solution for Catholics laboring under canon 915 as a result of their irregular marital status. As recently as 1994, the highest levels of Church authority have deliberately and unambiguously rejected internal forum solutions in cases of irregular marriage situations (see *Letter on Reception of Communion by Divorced and Remarried Catholics,* Congregation of the Doctrine of the Faith, September 14, 1994). The fact that so many Catholics are apparently using "internal forum solutions" to resolve their marital status problems based on the advice of priests and other spiritual counselors might well lessen their responsibility for having applied an inappropriate solution to their situation, but it still does not make their solution correct.

Question 85: **With divorce rates so high, and many Catholics seeking annulments, what prevents a divorced couple from just making up a story in order to get their annulment? How can Church officials verify what really happened in a marriage?**

Even though an annulment is a religious pronouncement, nullity petitions are still conducted in a legal context and must meet certain well-established canonical requirements before being declared. First, canon 1060 states that marriage "enjoys the favor of law." In other words, marriage, whether it be strictly Catholic, more broadly Christian, generally believing, or simply pagan, is presumed valid. A mere request for annulment is not sufficient to get one, even if both former spouses desire it. Instead, the marriage must be proved under canon law to be invalid (1983 CIC 1526).

Moreover, not only is a marriage itself generally considered valid, but the various elements that go into a marriage are given the benefit of the doubt. For example, persons are presumed capable of marriage unless prohibited by law (1983 CIC 1058) and the consent of the mind is presumed to be in accord with the words said at the wedding (1983 CIC 1101 § 1). All of these add up to impressive burdens of proof on those who would have a marriage declared null.

Second, canon 1608 requires the tribunal, if it finds for nullity, to have reached that decision with "moral certitude." This is the canonical version, though not simply the equivalent, of the civil law standard of "beyond a reasonable doubt." Canon 1608 means that it is not enough to show that a marriage could have been null or even that it was more likely null than not. Instead, the judges must be deeply assured that nullity has been proven in accord with the requirements of canon law.

As suggested by your question, of course, there remains the possibility of collusion between the parties. Indeed, some marriage nullity cases stand or fall based on information known only to the parties themselves. Because the Church does not have the same kind of physical and financial resources to compel truthfulness in its tribunals as do civil courts (but see 1983 CIC 1391 on the crime of falsehood), the Church frankly does rely more on the cooperation and integrity of the participants to arrive at accurate decisions. This is not as unreasonable as a cynical age might think, since in the great majority of nullity petitions, there are only religiously inspired motives at work in the first place. But even the most sincere parties can still be mistaken regarding their evidence.

At least two additional canonical institutions serve, as it were, to monitor the accuracy of tribunal decisions. First, a Defender of the Bond participates in every nullity petition passing before a diocesan tribunal. His or her task is to make sure that all reasonable arguments against declaring matrimonial nullity have been considered by the tribunal. Second, again because of the seriousness with which the Church defends the value of marriage, every case in which a marriage is declared null by a diocesan tribunal is automatically appealed to a higher court— again, regardless of the opinions of the parties or even of the Defender of the Bond (1983 CIC 1682). An entirely independent tribunal must agree that the annulment was properly declared before it becomes official.

Question 86: I have been told that I actually need two annulments before I can get married again. But I was only married once. What is going on?

I assume that when you say you were married only once, you do not have in mind the so-called "marriage that does not count" situation. For reasons explained elsewhere, there is no such thing as a marriage that does not count, and if this is what the tribunal is concerned about in your case, then you really do need two annulments.

More likely though, what you have been told has to do with a special rule in canon law applying only to marriage nullity cases. Briefly, every decision by a diocesan tribunal that results in a declaration of matrimonial nullity must be appealed to a higher ecclesiastical court (1983 CIC 1682 § 2). Known technically as "appeal by law," this rule applies even if both parties to the marriage want the annulment and even if the Defender of the Bond has no objections to the declaration of nullity. It is, therefore, only when the higher court, known as "second instance," agrees with the first court that a marriage has been proven null that the parties to that marriage are considered free of the marriage bond.

There is no additional fee for an "appeal by law" hearing, and in most, but not all, cases the first court's decision is confirmed by the higher court. If the second instance court does not agree with the first court's declaration of nullity, then depending on certain procedural facts, the case might be returned to the first court for reconsideration, or either or both parties could appeal the negative decision of second instance to the Roman Rota. Those options are usually explained only in the event they are needed, because of the complexities involved.

Usually a second instance process is conducted by tribunal personnel, although the parties to the marriage are informed about what is happening in the case, should they wish to take a more active part. Only in difficult cases would either or both parties be called upon to supply additional information to the higher court.

Question 87: What is a "marriage that doesn't count"?

As the phrase usually crops up in tribunal practice, it is a seriously misleading conclusion derived from some otherwise correct canonical principles. In brief, there is no such thing as a marriage that "doesn't count." Some examples might help. *Example 1:* A Catholic teenager bound by canonical form runs off to Las Vegas and marries before a justice of the peace. A few weeks later the couple splits up, and they get a civil divorce. Several years later, though, this Catholic wishes to marry in the Church.

Example 2: A Catholic, free to marry, attempts in good faith to marry someone whom, unbeknownst to the Catholic, is already validly married. The truth gets out, and a civil divorce follows quickly. Later this Catholic wishes to marry validly.

Both of these earlier attempts at marriage are so obviously likely to be null (1983 CIC 1108, 1085) that they would probably qualify for what canon law calls a "documentary process." This is a process that can result in an annulment without the necessity of a full tribunal trial (1983 CIC 1686). Here, though, is where the mistake can occur.

Recognizing the hollowness of the first attempt at marriage, one might be tempted to treat it as a "marriage that did not count" and simply not report it to the minister or tribunal. Maybe this information is withheld out of embarrassment, or to save time, or to spare the new intended spouse of ever knowing of the potentially painful past. But these are not reasons for nondisclosure; they are excuses, and they can be a recipe for disaster. How?

First, not every "open and shut" case qualifies for the quicker documentary procedure. Only the tribunal can make that determination. Second, not every nullity case, whether documentary or formal, results in a declaration of nullity. Again, only a Church court can make that determination. Third, every relationship, including an invalid marriage, leaves its mark on a person. Sometimes, moreover, the factors that led to an earlier invalid attempt at marriage might still be at work in a person. These factors should, maybe even must, be addressed before potentially repeating the same kinds of mistakes. This growth process, however, cannot be initiated if the past remains hidden.

For these and other reasons, canon law forbids a "second" marriage before the invalidity of the "first" is officially established (1983 CIC 1085). Please note that, strictly speaking, canon 1085, if violated, does not doom the "second" marriage to invalidity. Nevertheless, persons considering marriage under these circumstances, or perhaps persons already married thereunder, should not hesitate to discuss the facts honestly with a priest or canon lawyer and thereby receive advice on how to address these matters correctly.

Question 88: Do some people get more than one annulment?

Although not typical, neither is it unheard of for someone to obtain more than one declaration of nullity. This could happen in a couple of ways. For example, a petitioner might present several serial marriages for adjudication all at once. Or, less often but more disturbingly, some years after getting an annulment in order to enter a second marriage, a petitioner might return seeking annulment of that second marriage, perhaps even in order to enter yet a third. In any case, the reason for the multiplicity of annulments can be surprisingly simple: the factors which lead to the invalidity of marriage number 1, if left unresolved, could still have been at work, and hence destroyed the validity of marriage number 2, or number 3, and so on. If this sounds to you like a vicious circle, all I can say is that it sounds that way to me too. Unfortunately, when push comes to shove, canon law gives local Church authorities surprisingly little to prevent that scenario.

Question 89: **Are there too many annulments?**

Yes, far too many. But let us be clear about what we mean here. America's annulment picture—whether in terms of raw numbers, percentage of affirmative decisions, or in comparison with the rest of the world—is nothing to be proud of. If America still functions administratively, it does so despite Americans becoming increasingly dysfunctional (not to overuse a term) on a personal level. In declaring well over fifty-thousand marriages (not all of them Catholic or even American, by the way) null each year, America might be like the cancer-stricken oncologist—smart enough to diagnose its own matrimonial illnesses but too weak to cure itself. For cases involving a Catholic wedding, each annulment represents another example of where canon 1066—which calls for the elimination of anything which can affect the validity or licitness of a wedding before the ceremony—was honored too late. Each annulment, without a doubt, represents a personal human tragedy for all involved. An annulment is sometimes presented as the first step on the road to recovery in the life of faith, and often it is. But whatever else it might be, an annulment is primarily proof of a defeat—perhaps a self-inflicted or socially preconditioned defeat, but a defeat nevertheless. But let us be clear about what we mean here. In answering yes to the question of whether there are too many annulments, one needs to push the question back one step: What we need to ask is not, why there are so many annulments, but instead, why are there so many invalid marriages?

Question 90: **I know of a case in which the wife absolutely knocked herself out trying to save her marriage, and her husband, who was a real creep, got an annulment. How is that fair?**

Some people sincerely, but very mistakenly, view marriage as something like a tennis doubles team in which the strengths of one player can compensate for the weaknesses of the other player to such a degree that the team wins in the end. But things seldom work out that way in tennis, and, strictly speaking they never work out that way in marriage. Put me on a doubles court with a Wimbledon champ, and we would get whipped by any pair of decent players. Why? Because Wimbledon champs cannot play tennis? No, because *I* can't. The champ could complain all day long that he or she understood tennis, played well, deserved to be on a winning team, and so on. But we would still lose. Marriage, like doubles tennis, requires two people —not one, not one and a-half, but two complete, albeit fallen people. Canon law is very clear: *Both* spouses must be capable of and willing to enter marriage as the Church understands and proclaims it (1983 CIC 1057). The "super" capacity or commitment of one partner cannot be given to the other, even though we all know that no two spouses are equal, let alone identical, in their total ability or willingness to make a marriage work. Moreover, the mutual capacity and consent must be present on the wedding day, for Church law does not allow for post-wedding maturation to supply retroactively for pre-wedding deficiencies.

Question 91: I've been told that one of my two marriages is a "DF" case. What is a "DF"?

"DF" stands for *defect of canonical form*. At the time of your DF wedding, either you, your spouse, or both of you were Catholic and thus bound by the requirements of canonical form (see 1983 CIC 1108, 1117). Apparently that form was not observed, or it was only incompletely observed, at the time of the wedding, and hence that attempt at marriage must be declared null, probably by using an abbreviated tribunal procedure under canon 1686. While canonists technically distinguish between *lack of form* and *defect of form* cases, both types of cases, if proven, result in nullity as far as the spouses are concerned. Do not make the mistake many people do, though, and assume that a DF case is not really an annulment. It most certainly is. The process for declaring nullity in such cases might be expedited and it might be less costly, but DF cases remain declarations of nullity. Indeed, roughly 25 percent of all the annulments declared each year in the United States are DF annulments. They therefore contribute in a startling way to the explosion of annulments in America.

Question 92: I was born and raised Catholic, but I fell away from the Church while a young adult and joined an evangelical Protestant church. During that time, I got married and later divorced. I had a vague feeling that I should have gotten the Catholic Church's permission to marry, but because I was active in that other church, I let it slide. I've since come back to the Catholic Church, but I'm getting conflicting stories about my chances for an annulment. Some say that because I wasn't married in a Catholic ceremony, my marriage is automatically null, others have told me that the rules have changed and my former marriage might be valid. What's the story?

Your question boils down to whether or not you were bound by canonical form at the time of your wedding. If your wedding took place on or before November 26, 1983—that is, before the 1983 Code took effect—you were almost certainly bound by canonical form and, having evidently not observed it, your attempt at marriage was probably null under Church law.

But if your wedding took place on or after November 27, 1983, there is a good chance you were not bound by canonical form, in light of a new canon that exempts from the obligation of form those Catholics "who have left the Church by a formal act" (1983 CIC 1117). While the code does not define "formal act of defection," it is certainly speaking of something more than just "falling away" from the faith, as you admit to doing. Joining a Protestant denomination and actively participating in it, on the other hand, will probably qualify as a formal act of defection. If so, you were not bound to observe Catholic form at the time of your wedding, and your failure to have done so will not automatically result in the canonical nullity of your marriage.

Only a diocesan tribunal can render a judgment on the above scenarios, and you should certainly present the information as accurately as possible to the tribunal to help it arrive at a reliable conclusion on the issues. Do not make the mistake of considering this a "marriage that didn't count" and simply forgetting about it. If it turns out that you were not bound by form and hence that you cannot use that as the basis of impugning your marriage, you (or your former spouse, for that matter) will still be allowed to raise issues concerning matrimonial capacity and consent as possible bases for nullity. Again, though, only a diocesan tribunal can adjudicate those issues for you.

Question 93: **When I went into my first marriage, I did so with serious doubts that I was doing to right thing. I knew my ex-husband had been married before and that there was no annulment of that marriage. I went ahead with the wedding, though, because I figured that if things didn't work out, we could get divorced and I could apply for an annulment because of my ex's former marriage. I realize this sounds rather calculating, but was my thinking about the annulment correct?**

If you are looking for a simple, albeit grudging yes, I can't give you one. Canon law, and the Church it serves, has been around a long time. Schemes like yours are not new, and the Code has provisions that apply in cases like this. First, the impediment of *ligamen*, or prior marriage bond, that you are counting on to deprive your former spouse of matrimonial capacity (1983 CIC 1085) only arises from a valid marriage. Now, while the Church generally presumes the validity of marriages that more or less look like marriages, it retains the authority to investigate virtually any marriage, including those whose validity directly affects the possible validity of a later marriage. If the tribunal from which you are seeking the annulment of your marriage doubts the validity of your ex-husband's first marriage (and the Defender of the Bond and the Promoter of Justice are just the types to raise such questions if they choose), there would be no moral certitude about his being bound by *ligamen*.

So you try your second theory of nullity, which runs thus: *Even if my ex-spouse was not validly married, I thought he was. So when I consented to marriage, I did not think it would be a valid marriage, and therefore I consented invalidly* (1983 CIC 1057 § 2). Maybe, maybe not. Canon 1100, hiding way back in the provisions on consent, says that the knowledge or opinion of the nullity of a marriage does not necessarily prevent matrimonial consent from being given (see also 1983 CIC 1107). In other words, the mere fact (assuming it can be proven) that you reasonably felt your marriage would be invalid does not necessarily mean that the consent you gave to that marriage is invalid. It might have been, and you would be allowed to try to prove it. But it is not the canonical cakewalk you, and others before you, have predicted. You would have to prove, among other things, that but for your opinion of nullity, you would not have given your consent at all to your marriage. Perhaps you can prove this; but your already being engaged at the time you came up with this idea is going to give the Defender of the Bond some basis for challenging your claims on this point.

Now, do not misunderstand. You have the same rights as anyone else to impugn your marriage, and even though your particular theories of nullity might not pan out as you hoped, you have, whether you know it or not, given other signs of possible nullity in your marriage. The point is merely this: Be honest and accurate in your depiction of events, and let the tribunal determine whether you have presented a recognizable basis for nullity and, if so, whether you have produced sufficient evidence to prove your claim. Do not try to outwit the tribunal.

Question 94: **Will the tribunal speed up an annulment case because a pregnant woman needs it in order to get remarried in the Church?**

No. That simply sows the seeds of doubt about the woman's discretion of judgment (1983 CIC 1095, n.2) or submission to reverential fear (1983 CIC 1103) in entering a second marriage. It has taken awhile, but we are finally getting to the point where social pressures to wed in response to a premarital pregnancy are fading. The last thing most diocesan tribunals want to do is encourage more such frequently shortsighted decisions. Even though a tribunal could take a case like the one you are describing out of turn, there would be little prudence in its doing so. And the chances of its doing so are very slim.

Question 95: **Prior to our civil marriage, my wife and I had both been married and divorced. We stopped receiving the sacraments after we got married to each other, although we still went to Mass. Since then, we both applied for annulments of our earlier marriages. My wife's annulment has already come through and I am told that mine will shortly. We plan to have our marriage blessed in the Church as soon as we can after that. Is our getting the annulments and having our marriage blessed all we need to do in order to be readmitted to the sacraments?**

Whatever the factors that led you and your present spouse to marry outside of the Church, it is clear that you take the rest of the Church's sacramental life seriously and that you are sincerely trying to rectify your matrimonial status in the Church. Assuming things go as you have said, I would think the following. Your annulment and your spouse's mean that the Church considers you to be single people free to marry each other. While it is often impractical for civilly married but canonically single people such as yourselves to separate (for example, there might be small children to care for), you should not, precisely as single people, make use of marital privileges (specifically, sexual intercourse).

With the "blessing of your marriage," known technically as a *convalidation* (1983 CIC 1156, 1160), the Church would consider you a married couple. From that point on, of course, there would be no moral bar to the exercise of marital rights nor any canonical bar to sacramental participation based on your marital status.

But here is what I would invite you to think about: For a period of time in the past, you and your spouse were consciously in an invalid marriage ("living in sin," as some put it). While your annulments and convalidation put an end to this irregular situation, it does not erase it. Christ does that, usually in confession. Canon 1065 § 2 strongly recommends that all those who are about to be married go to confession and receive Holy Eucharist. You and your spouse seem especially receptive to these opportunities for grace and growth, and I encourage you to talk with a spiritual director or confessor about what is best in your situation.

Question 96: **Before getting married, my ex-husband and I entered into a pre-nuptial contract in which we agreed, in the event of a divorce, not to contest each other's request for an annulment. Now he has broken that agreement and is fighting my nullity petition. What should I expect the diocesan tribunal to do about that?**

Nothing. Such contracts have absolutely no force under canon law. Indeed, I cannot imagine a Catholic minister officiating at a wedding if he knew that such a promise on future annulments had been made (1983 CIC 1066). Ironically perhaps, the fact that such a contract was even made raises, in my mind, certain questions about the sufficiency of the consent you exchanged at your wedding (see, for example, 1983 CIC 1101 § 2, 1102 § 1), but it will be for the tribunal to assess that matter in much more detail than is possible here. The mere fact that such a contract was made, I should say, would not automatically invalidate the marriage, although the tribunal will want to know about it and will want to consider what it might have portended concerning the parties' attitude toward the permanence of marriage.

Question 97: **I have real problems with the Church's claim to be able to annul marriages. I don't see that in the Bible anywhere. What I do see is: "What God has joined, let no man put asunder." Please comment.**

Generally, I let imprecisions in a question pass because such imprecisions do not usually affect the answer. But they might in this case. The Church does not claim the power to annul marriages if by that you mean the power to transform something that was into something that is not. An annulment case, assuming it "goes affirmative," is the Church's official declaration that what seemed to have been a valid marriage was not one. I understand that this is a distinction that is hard for some people to make and that a generally cynical age might dismiss as "hocus-pocus." Well, and no disrespect intended, that is their problem. In the meantime, it is simply wrong to attribute to the Church a power that it denies it even has (1983 CIC 1141). There are many instances in which the Church is called upon to defend powers that it uses, if only in the court of public opinion. But in the case of annulments, no specific power is being used against a marriage. On the contrary, as is true for every advanced society, the Church has a mechanism for investigating the actual binding nature of the commitments (or *apparent* commitments) made among its members. These investigations do not negate the power of people to commit themselves to a certain status; rather these procedures are used to determine whether that power was in fact employed in a specific instance.

The above said, there are a few (very few) types of valid marriages that can be dissolved (*not* annulled) under certain circumstances. Marriages that were never consummated, for example, represent one kind of case in which dissolution might be possible (1983 CIC 1142). Likewise, a marriage of a previously unbaptized person could under certain circumstances, be dissolved by a second marriage (but *not* by the Church) if it serves the Christian life of the newly baptized spouse (see 1983 CIC 1143, 1147). Note, though, that in these latter cases, the source of the practice is not so much canon law, but St. Paul's teaching in 1 Corinthians 7:12-15. This is known as the *Pauline Privilege.*

Question 98: **I understand that I need an annulment before I can enter the Church, but I have been told that the backlog of cases is two years, sometimes three. Why should I be kept waiting that long?**

No one is happy with tribunal backlogs, and they can cause people real hardship. Despite canons that encourage nullity cases to be processed within one and a half years (see 1983 CIC 1453), backlogs of cases beyond those time limits do exist. You have a couple options.

If the case is a very solid one with excellent supporting testimony, you or your advocate could ask that it be taken out of turn, especially if resolution of the case is necessary for entrance into the Church or con-validation of an otherwise apparently stable family relationship (1983 CIC 1458). Understand that many petitions might meet this standard, though, and that the tribunal need not grant your petition for an expedited hearing. Alternatively, it is possible that other tribunals, if they are equally competent to hear the case, could be approached to accept the case under certain circumstances.

In any case, do not try to come into the Church until your marital status is settled, even if a well-intentioned pastor is willing to accept you because "it is not your fault that your open-and-shut case cannot be heard for some time." Not all "open-and-shut" cases really are "open-and-shut," and there is also the chance that certain restrictions on a future marriage might be imposed by the tribunal. Besides, as long as one is in an irregular union, one simply is not eligible for full sacramental participation (1983 CIC 205, 915). Having correctly seen the value of Church membership, do not let your entrance into the Church be cheapened by coming in irregularly.

Question 99: **You quoted canon law a lot in your answers. Can lay people have copies of canon law?**

Certainly. Useful English versions of current canon law include the following: *Code of Canon Law/Latin-English Edition: New English Translation*, published by the Canon Law Society of America; and *The Code of Canon Law in English Translation*, published by William B. Eerdmans. Each of these is available from or ordered through your local Catholic bookstore. Likewise, there are translations of the 1983 Code available in nearly every major modern language.

Question 100: **Our neighbors were divorced a few years back, and recently the marriage was annulled because the wife was pregnant at the time of their wedding. This has greatly upset me because I was pregnant when I got married, too, but I feel perfectly fine in my marriage. Am I living in a null marriage?**

Your marriage is presumptively valid (1983 CIC 1060), but your question illustrates well the dangers of incomplete, even erroneous, understandings about how the annulment process works. Pregnancy at the time of marriage is not grounds for an annulment. Your neighbor's marriage was annulled only because the tribunal system found with moral certainty that one or both of the parties to that marriage suffered from invalidating flaws in matrimonial capacity, consent, or form. If pregnancy is relevant to a nullity petition (and it often is), this is only because that condition sheds light on other serious problems dooming the marriage before it ever started. My wife went to the dentist last week. When she came back, she told me the dentist had found a cavity. Now, we eat the same foods, we observe the same dental hygiene, we are the same age, and so on, and I am going to the same dentist next week. My wife's experience does not doom me to having a cavity, does it? People should never try to analyze their marriage situation based on the experiences of similarly situated family or friends. If someone has a question about the canonical status of his or her marriage, especially if the marriage is intact, it is a good idea to seek qualified advice. But he or she should do as the Church does: presume the validity of their marriage.

ANNULMENTS IN AMERICA: KEEPING BAD NEWS IN CONTEXT

Prefatory Note: Since this article first appeared in 1996, it has been viewed both by its many supporters and by its few detractors as a defense of American tribunal practice. Actually, it is no such thing. My goal is simply to point out that criticisms of American tribunals based on statistics, regardless of where such criticism arose, are open to rebuttal, for the simple reason that all statistical measurements of institutional activity need to be understood in a wider context. My article has clearly met that goal. As one highly orthodox and highly placed reader told me, "I read your piece with care, and am at last persuaded that the situation is not as catastrophic as I had feared." Even those who are stridently opposed to my arguments found themselves contextualizing tribunal statistics in their arguments (not always persuasively, in my opinion, but at least in a way that conceded the need to appreciate the wider contexts in which annulment statistics are generated.) I count that as a small victory, as one step toward the truth that will set all men free.

Of course, even if a host of reasonable people found all of my arguments persuasive, that would not necessarily mean that tribunals (American, Roman, or any others) are conducting their cases correctly. They still might be liable to serious criticism. Conversely, even if all of my arguments were defeated, that would not prove tribunals are acting wrongly. They still might be arriving at just decisions. If we can agree to recognize tribunal statistics for what they are, not reading too much or too little into them, and avoid becoming mired in them as if they and they alone tell the story of the crisis in married life— itself closely connected to the general crisis in the West—then we will be better able to move to the more important and more substantive catechetical, doctrinal, moral, social, and psychological issues that must be addressed if Church teaching on marriage is to have its salvific effect in the lives of the faithful. As did Pope John Paul II, I hold that there are too many annulments in America (and in Canada, in France, in South Africa, and in Rome as well). I hope that my writing and my work lead to a state wherein, justly, there will be many fewer annulments, many, many fewer divorces, and ever fewer doomed-from-the-outset attempts at pseudo-marriage.

Thoughtful Americans are disturbed at the high number of divorces in the United States. But some observers look at the concomitantly sharp rise in declarations of matrimonial nullity (commonly called *annulments*) being granted by American diocesan tribunals and suggest, if not conclude, that U.S. tribunals are capitulating to the divorce mentality, perhaps even fanning its flames.

The criticisms made against American tribunals spring from a wide variety of sources and take a wide variety of forms. Too numerous to cite here, these sources of criticism include Vatican officials, heterodox and orthodox clerics and laity, and virtually all major organs of Catholic opinion. The criticisms offered by these disparate sources include: annulments are being granted too quickly, they are not being granted quickly enough, tribunals overuse the consent canons as a basis for nullity, they are only scratching the surface of the consent canons in nullity cases, annulments are only for the rich, annulments are wasting diocesan resources, and so on. Serving, however, as the fire which keeps this hot pot of debate boiling is the tremendous surge in American annulment activity. In most fields, of course, raw numbers and their ratios are only used as measures of institutional activity. But in the annulment context, tribunal statistics themselves are often used, consciously or otherwise, as actual criticisms of tribunal activity. These criticisms are posed by means of what I call the "numbers stick."

The statistically-oriented "numbers stick" generally takes one of three forms: 1) the great rise in the total number of American annulments means that there is something wrong with U.S. tribunals; 2) the relatively high ratio of affirmative decisions granted in America means that there is something wrong with

U.S. tribunals; and 3) the generally disproportionate tribunal activity in America means that there is something wrong with U.S. tribunals. This article will examine the "numbers stick" to see how it fares under rebuttal.

I. Total numbers

In the early 1960s, about three hundred declarations of nullity came from the United States each year; today that annual figure has grown to over sixty thousand.[1] By any measure, that is a staggering increase. But is this huge increase in annulments a sign of tribunal laxity toward marriage or complicity in its demise? Consider: during the same decades in which declarations of matrimonial nullity were soaring in the United States, similarly huge increases in, for example, product liability awards and successful prosecutions for child abuse were experienced in the civil arena. Are these phenomena, however, taken as proof of dysfunction in the American legal system? Not usually. Rather, they are the direct result of major changes made in the underlying civil laws governing such cases, changes which not only made some kinds of jury awards and criminal convictions more likely, but which in turn encouraged more cases to be filed under the revised laws.[2] Similarly, some very significant changes in canonical procedure have been made over the last thirty years, changes which facilitated both the filing of marriage nullity petitions and the chances that such petitions will be proven. But these changes, being technical in nature, tended to pass unnoticed by the average tribunal observer. To take just one example, until 1969, canon law basically allowed annulment petitions to be filed only in the diocese in which the wedding was celebrated or in the diocese in which the respondent (the other party to the marriage) currently lived.[3] But beginning in 1970, the Holy See approved for use in the United

States a modified canonical procedure which allowed petitioners to file their nullity cases in the diocese in which they currently lived, regardless of where the wedding was celebrated or where their ex-spouse now lived.[3] The implications of this one canonical change in a country like America were enormous.

Recall that, not only are Americans generally prone to be mobile over the years, but marital failure accelerates and compounds this predilection in that divorcees are even more apt to change their surroundings as part of starting a new life. Since 1970, however, divorced Catholics are no longer required by canon law to return to the place of their wedding or to the territory of their former spouse in order to have their petition for nullity heard. The petitioner, always a motivated and knowledgeable party, can now have his or her petition heard in the most convenient tribunal.[4]

Tribunal competence was just one area in which canonical procedures were significantly revised by Rome in ways that facilitated matrimonial nullity filings and declarations. Other procedural changes included allowing a single judge to hear a case instead of requiring three judges to hear each petition, and eliminating caps on the number of qualified judges allowed to serve in a diocese; eliminating restrictions which prevented "guilty" spouses from seeking annulments, and allowing non-Catholics to file cases in diocesan tribunals; eliminating several of the more archaic regulations on the types of evidence allowed and the numbers of witnesses needed in nullity cases; and imposing new, or shortening old, time limits for the speedier treatment of marriage cases. Each of these Roman changes in procedural canon law have indisputably contributed to the dramatic increase in declarations of marriage nullity.[5]

As important as were the procedural changes above, they combined in potent fashion with the Roman decision to include in the 1983 Code a single new norm on marriage consent, namely canon 1095. Of the fifteen or twenty possible grounds upon which a marriage case can be heard (1983 CIC 1083–1105), more nullity petitions are adjudicated on the basis of canon 1095 than on all the others combined.[6] Canon 1095 of the revised Code, without precedent in the 1917 Code, is the single canon which most directly allows tribunals to address the canonical impact of mental, emotional, personal, psychological, psychiatric, and even chemical traumas suffered by persons attempting marriage.

Like most first attempts at legislating on complex areas, canon 1095 suffers, I think, from certain conceptual problems and has been subject to various schools of interpretation whose analysis is beyond the scope of this article. Here I have limited the discussion to the statistically-oriented complaints against U.S. tribunals. But the fundamental insight of canon 1095 is crucial in helping the Church confront accurately the modern crises in marriage. Canon 1095, for all its flaws, is still the best tool for addressing cases in which drug and alcohol abuse, physical or sexual abuse, psychological and psychiatric anomalies, and a variety of other mental and emotional conditions have seriously impacted parties prior to marriage.

Frankly, to attack American tribunals on the basis that, under canon 1095, they are declaring null tens of thousands more marriages than they did a few decades ago is akin to attacking American hospitals on the basis that they are diagnosing tens of thousands more cases of HIV/AIDS than they did a few decades ago. This analogy might be unfair in that HIV/AIDS apparently did not exist thirty years ago, whereas fallen human nature and divorce did. Nevertheless, no credible social observer takes the position that average levels of personal maturity or individual integrity— two very important factors in canon 1095 cases—have done anything but plummet over the last thirty years.

Consider: Most tribunal critics recognize well the profound truth of the Church teachings contained in *Humanae Vitae.* Yet I see no acknowledgment by tribunal critics that the wholesale disregard for, or ignorance of, those teachings among lay Catholics (to say nothing of non-Catholics coming before diocesan tribunals) is having any significant impact on the attempts of such people to enter marriage. The use of contraceptives, even abortifacients, is not a canonical impediment to marriage but, whether as cause or effect, it seems highly correlative of the startling, and ultimately destructive, levels of immaturity and irresponsibility which so many people try to bring to marriage today. For that matter, stories of heterodox, including pro-contraceptive marriage preparation programs and sex education classes are legion. Cannot such programs (some of them in place for over twenty years now) be having exactly the kind of grave anti-family/anti-marriage effects that opponents rightly fear?

Before leaving the topic of the huge increase in the basic number of annulments declared in the U.S., one final but very important point should be considered: namely, the effect of canonical form requirements on annulment numbers. This requirement of canonical form is what causes "Las Vegas style" weddings to be invalid for Catholics; indeed, such weddings are so obviously canonically invalid that they qualify for a faster documentary process for declaring such marriages null.[7] But, second only to annulments based on canon 1095, more U.S. annulments are based on violations of canonical form than on any other cause. In 1991, for example, nearly 18,700 of the 63,900 American declarations of nullity were based on violations of canonical form.[8]

Tribunal judges have virtually no discretion in the handling of canonical form cases; it is as close to an utterly objective type of case as canon law has.[9] And yet canonical form cases consistently account for up to twenty-five percent of all the annulments being granted in America.[10] Even if, therefore, one were to argue that American tribunals consistently misinterpret the psychological canons on consent, one is still left having to account for the huge number of canonical form nullity cases, whose numbers, standing alone, still dwarf the total number of pre-APN annulments declared in the U.S.

II. Percentage of affirmatives

The second category of "numbers stick" criticism concedes the irrelevance of the increase in raw numbers of annulments, but argues that the ratio of affirmative decisions to petitions is so high as to support a suspicion of pervasive "anti-marriage/pro-nullity" biases on the part of most tribunal judges. The criticism is commonly put: American tribunals nullify ninety-five percent of the marriages that come before them. The first time I heard this criticism, I conceded the accuracy of the percentage (something I would not do today, for the reasons discussed below.) But I then asked the critic whether he considered American municipal courts generally fair in their treatment of the cases which come before them. We both agreed that such courts are generally considered fair and effective, at which point I observed that the conviction rate of defendants in such courts usually exceeds ninety percent. While no one wants to equate traffic tickets with broken families, the comparison does suggest a danger in forming conclusions about the fairness of courts, or tribunals, based solely on the way the majority of cases are decided in such fora.[11]

Today, however, I would dispute the percentage of annulments which some claim are being granted. But to understand this rebuttal one must have a basic grasp of the major stages in processing a marriage case.

Virtually every nullity petition resulting in an affirmative tribunal decision begins as an interview in a pastor's office. This is a practically useful, though technically unofficial, part of most tribunals' procedures, and hence is not given to close monitoring. And yet, while most pastors (or their staffs) are very willing to assist potential petitioners in drafting their forms for the tribunal, it also happens that some potential petitioners are dissuaded from filing their petitions based on discussions with their pastor or his staff. This is usually because the pastor has stated or hinted at his opinion that the case "probably won't be approved by the tribunal." My hunch (and that is all I have on this point) is that those pastors are usually right. The petition probably would have been a weak one, and it probably would not have been approved in a formal trial.

Assuming completion of the parish-based paperwork, potential petitions are forwarded to the diocesan tribunal. In a preliminary procedure, these petitions are examined for routine things like the presence of necessary supporting documents such as baptismal and wedding certificates, divorce decrees, etc. Here again, though, the opportunity arises for tribunal personnel to suggest either to the pastor or directly to the potential petitioner withdrawing the petition because of what appear to be factors which typically prevent an affirmative decision. Being the recommendation of canonical experts, such informal suggestions are even more likely to be on point, resulting in again more weak cases being eliminated before officially entering the tribunal system.

Even after official acceptance of a petition, however, it can happen that a petitioner loses interest in the case, or witnesses fail to come forward in a useful manner, or other factors emerge which prevent the case from moving forward. Almost invariably, a petition which "stalls" does so for the same types of reasons which would have resulted, had the case gone to sentence, in its being denied. With these major, if not always official, stages in mind, let's examine some of the statistics on apparent affirmative rates in U.S. tribunals.

In 1991 some 48,600 petitions were considered as presented to American tribunals.[12] Of those, only 43,900 were accepted for adjudication and, of those, only about 39,100 were decided by formal sentences. Assume that almost all of these sentences were affirmative. That is still only an 89 percent affirmative rate among cases actually accepted, and barely eighty percent for those cases officially presented. Moreover, the affirmative rate drops even more when one recalls that additional weak cases are weeded out at the parish level or perhaps presented only in part to the tribunal and some cases go negative.

One could, I suppose, maintain that even this eighty percent affirmative rate is too high—although how one could hold this opinion without examining individual cases escapes me. It might be worth comparing the U.S. affirmative rate with Rome's, specifically the Roman Rota's.

According to Augustine Mendonca's recently published Rotal Anthology, during, for example, the three years surrounding the promulgation of the revised Code of Canon Law, 1982 through 1984, the Roman Rota heard 571 cases dealing with matrimonial nullity, and reached an affirmative result in 354 of them, for a sixty-two percent affirmative rate.[13] Certainly no one I know accuses the Roman Rota of being soft on marriage cases. While Rome's apparent sixty-two percent affirmative rate is not as high as America's apparent eighty percent rate, neither is it as low as some might think.

Of course, any number of factors might have influenced the Rota's affirmative percentage—things like taking cases from around the world, or like its serving extensively as an appellate court—and such factors should be considered in assessing the Rota's performance. But cannot procedural or demographic factors affect American tribunal performance, too? In any event, some recognition that over half of the marriage cases handled by the Roman Rota apparently end in an affirmative sentence seems in order.[14]

Finally, to the degree that percentages are relevant at all, one might ask what percentage of divorced Catholics in America have actually received a declaration of nullity. Speculation on this point is hampered because there do not appear to be firm figures on just how many divorced (albeit perhaps remarried) Catholics there are in America.[15]

But reasonable estimates on the percentage of divorced Catholics in America who have received a declaration of nullity range anywhere from five to twenty-five percent. I'll go with ten percent and ask: is that ratio really too high?

Should we not expect the Church's teaching on marriage, which is reflected in its canon law, to shed some light on the causes of modern matrimonial collapse? In every ten failed Catholic marriages, should we be surprised that at least one of those marriages failed for the very reasons which Church law itself tried to warn would result in invalidity?

Or are we to hold that the canon law on marriage—and the Church teaching it upholds—is so irrelevant to modern married life that its disregard by couples will have no actual impact on their lives and marriages in this world? Or, on the other hand, does a couple's demonstrable respect for the Church's marriage requirements offer no protection against the ravages of divorce? Ideally, of course, there ought to be no divorces and no annulments, but if there are to be civil divorces, canonical nullity should account for a significant percentage of those failed marriages.[16]

III. Disproportionate American activity

The third category of "numbers stick" criticism prescinds from the first two critiques outlined above, and focuses on the indisputably anomalous situation of American tribunals as compared to the rest of the world. This critique is often put: American Catholics make up five percent of the world's Catholic population, but they get eighty percent of the Catholic world's annulments.[17]

I frankly feel that this is the shallowest of all tribunal criticisms. Americans make up six percent of the world's population, but they account for 100 percent of the men on the moon. So what? America functions. Much of the rest of the world does not.

American tribunals keep sufficient and reliable office hours, their telephones work, their mail is delivered on time, and if their photocopy machine breaks down, replacement parts are not six months away. Most of the parties and witnesses in an American nullity case will be able to drive to the tribunal in their own car on a paved road without hindrance by anything from fuel shortages to partisans in civil wars. In an almost incalculable and invisible number of ways, American Catholics have the leisure, in the classical sense of the word, to worry about their juridic status in the Church. Do we really expect a plethora of nullity cases to be processed from Catholics in communist China, Bosnia, or some third-world drug republic?

Well, one might rejoin, what about those countries where a Hobbesian hell does not hold sway? For the most part, such countries are either industrialized Pacific rim nations like Japan, with virtually no Catholic population, or they are a western European country like France or the Netherlands with what, in comparison to the U.S., can fairly be called a notably apathetic Catholic population.

Ever since De Tocqueville penned his classic study of America, historians have recognized that the average American takes religious issues much more seriously than does the average European, and, moreover, that Americans are markedly more concerned about legal procedures, rights and duties. What people of what nation, therefore, would be more inclined by desire and more able in means than Americans to use a religious-legal procedure like annulments to assess their canonical status in their Church?

Of course, if one still wishes to criticize America for its disproportional tribunal activity, one could just as easily, and just as misleadingly, point out that Italy, with just five percent of the world's Catholic population, accounts for at least seventy percent of the Roman Rota's case load; indeed, the Rota grants more annulments to Italians than it does to the rest of the world combined.[18] But if one cannot take those patently disproportionate Italian figures and conclude that Rome is winking at marriage (even at Italian marriage), why should one be allowed to take America's similarly disproportionate annulment statistics and conclude that U.S. tribunals are lax in their administration of canonical justice?

I do not wish to be misunderstood: America's annulment picture, whether in terms of its raw numbers, its percentage of affirmative decisions, or in comparison with the rest of the world, is nothing to be proud of. Like a cancer-stricken oncologist, America might be smart enough to diagnose its own illnesses, but unable to cure itself.

Each annulment represents, without any hyperbole, a personal human tragedy, usually two human tragedies, and often several human tragedies combined. And, for those cases which involved a Catholic wedding, each annulment represents yet another example of where canon 1066—which calls the elimination of anything which can affect the validity or liceity of a wedding before the ceremony—was honored too late.[19]

The news on American annulments is bad, but that bad news should be kept in context. Most certainly, I do not take the position that American tribunals are above reproach in their handling of nullity cases, and some of the substantive, as opposed to statistical, criticisms of American tribunal practice do deserve closer attention.

But I am sure I'm not alone among tribunal personnel when I feel that modern American tribunals are still being held accountable for some of the rash statements made by some American canonists during the first heady days of American Procedural Norms. In any event, it serves no purpose to attack today's tribunals for, I think, accurately "diagnosing" the extent of the divorce disease among Americans.

Certainly, I have opinions on how we might come to grips with the on-going collapse of the American, and Catholic, family. Other people have theirs. Most of all, though, the Church has its grace and wisdom to apply. So, if this study only helps eliminate the less fruitful ideas for reform, especially the idea that there's nothing wrong with Catholic American marriages that can't be fixed by shutting down American diocesan tribunals, I shall be satisfied.

This is a slightly modified version of an article which first appeared in the November 1996 issue of Homiletic and Pastoral Review.

NOTES

1 See *The Code of Canon Law: A Text and Commentary*, (New York: Paulist, 1985), hereafter CLSA Commentary, at p. 1010, and *1994 Catholic Almanac* (Huntington, Indiana: Our Sunday Visitor), 236, reporting for the year 1991. Throughout this article, 1991 is chosen as a typical year because its data is widely available, but it falls several years after the promulgation of the 1983 Code of Canon Law, meaning that virtually all nullity cases heard now are being treated in light of the new law.

2 Some changes in American law are the result of judicial attitudes being substituted, rightly or wrongly, for legislative intent. But in canon law, such a feat is virtually impossible. The Code of Canon Law is replete with effective restrictions on the ability of anyone beside the legislator to change substantive or procedural law (see, for example, 1983 CIC 8, 16, 17, 19, 1404–1406 & 1417). Not even the Roman Rota can interpret canon law contrary to the Pope's intentions.

3 See "Provisional Norms for Marriage Annulment Cases in [the] United States," 28 April 1970, *Canon Law Digest*, VII 950–966. The "American Procedural Norms" had been drafted by the Canon Law Society of America in the mid to late 1960s and proposed for Roman approval by the National Conference of Catholic Bishops shortly later. Absent Roman authorization, the APN would have remained speculative exercises by academics; but after Roman approval, they became binding law in U.S. tribunals. Afterward, if an American tribunal judge, fearful that these new procedural norms would threaten the stability of marriage, had refused to accept a petition correctly filed under the APN, canon law itself would have threatened him with sanctions up to and including removal from office. (See 1917 CIC 1625, 6 1 and 1983 CIC 1457.) Many of the more "liberalizing" provisions of the APN were later made applicable throughout the Roman Catholic world as part of Pope Paul VI's apostolic letter

Causas matrimoniales, 28 March 1971, *Canon Law Digest*, VII 969–974, AAS 63–441.

4   The current law, 1983 CIC 1673, n. 3, differs from the APN only in requiring the consent of the respondent's judicial vicar, who in turn need only hear (not obtain the consent of) the respondent. Most requests for competence filed under 1673, n. 3, are approved because: a) most respondents do not in fact object to a "foreign" tribunal hearing their ex-spouse's petition; and b) the relatively few respondents who do object, usually object not to the hearing of the case in the diocese of their ex-spouse, but rather to any tribunal's hearing the case—something respondents clearly have no canonical right to assert.

5   The Holy See incorporated most of these APN-type provisions in the 1983 Code with full awareness of the impact such procedures were having on American nullity cases. The Canon Law Society of America had been reporting annually the explosion in American nullity cases regularly since the mid-1970s, and arguments against continuing the APN were raised by Roman dicasteries as early as 1973. See *Canon Law Digest*, VIII 1155–1157 & 1167–1169. Additional criticisms of the APN were raised by the Signatura in 1977 and in 1978, some five years before the 1983 Code took effect. See *Canon Law Digest*, IX 979–987 and *Canon Law Digest*, X 256–262. For a more recent Roman acknowledgement that the 1983 Code does increase the chances of proving invalid marriages null, see the appendix for the Congregation for the Doctrine of the Faith's Letter on "Reception of Communion: Divorced-and-Remarried Catholics," 14 September 1994, Para. 9, which states in part "The discipline of the Church, while it confirms the exclusive competence of ecclesiastical tribunals with respect to the examination of the validity of the marriage of Catholics, also offers new ways to demonstrate the nullity of a previous marriage in order to exclude as far as possible every divergence between the truth verifiable in the judicial process and the objective truth known by a correct conscience." More recently still, *Newsweek* reported (5 February 1996, p. 6) that the Pope has urged the Roman Rota "to get moving on its backlog of annulment requests."

6   This is not entirely due to the very broad scope of canon 1095. It is also because many of the grounds for nullity address fact situ-

ations which are very rarely encountered in America. We have, for example, hardly any 15 year old boys attempting church weddings (c. 1083) and very few kidnapped woman being forced to marry their captors (c. 1089). Likewise, "AWOL" priests and religious rarely come back and seek annulments of their marriages (cc. 1087 & 1088).

7   See generally 1983 CIC 1108, 1127 & 1686–1688.

8   See *1994 Catholic Almanac*, 236.

9   One could also consider so-called "ligamen" petitions, that is, cases in which nullity must be declared because at least one of the parties was shown already to be in a presumably valid marriage (1983 CIC 1085 ,6 1, eligible for expedited hearing under 1983 CIC 1686). In 1991, for example, over 2,200 American annulments were granted on the basis of ligamen, or prior bond, on the part of one or both parties to the impugned marriage. See "Tribunal Statistics Summary," *CLSA Proceedings* (1992), 252–268. Ironically, these annulments based on ligamen provided over 2,200 more times one could attack American tribunals for disregarding the sanctity of marriage, when in fact they were literally upholding it.

10   Rome might be reconsidering the automatic nullity implications of canonical form attendant to Catholic baptism. Canon 1117 now exempts from the requirement of canonical form Catholics "who have left the Church by a formal act." Presumably, somewhat fewer marriages involving Catholics can be declared null solely on the basis of lack of canonical form. But see appendix one for the Congregation for the Doctrine of the Faith's letter *On the Reception of Communion by Divorced and Remarried Catholics,* 14 September 1994, Para. 9, which states in part "Adherence to the Church's judgment and observance of the existing discipline concerning the obligation of canonical form necessary for the validity of the marriage of Catholics are what truly contribute to the spiritual welfare of the faithful concerned."

11   The population treated in diocesan tribunals and municipal courts is obviously relevant to, though not dispositive of, their conclusions on particular cases. Take the first hundred drivers

passing in front of one's house, and the first hundred drivers sitting in traffic court, and ask which group is more likely to contain a higher number of offenders. Likewise, take the first hundred families at a mall, and the first hundred arguing sets of spouses in divorce court (a civil divorce is a virtual prerequisite to filing a canonical petition for nullity), and ask which group is more likely to have more people in invalid marriages.

12 See "Tribunal Statistics Summary," *CLSA Proceedings* (1992), 252–268.

13 See A. Mendonca, *Rotal Anthology: An Annotated Index of Rotal Decisions from 1971 to 1988*, (Washington, DC: Canon Law Society of America, 1992), 755–769.

14 For the entire period 1971–1988, Mendonca lists 236 Rotal cases as coming from America, 127 (52%) of which went affirmative. See Mendonca, *Rotal Anthology*, 688–695. If, however, a tribunal critic were to try to take this lower figure and argue that only 50% of American annulment petitions would, after Rotal review, be considered as proven (for many reasons, this would be a difficult argument to make) that would still suggest that well over 30,000 U.S. declarations of nullity would be provable each year. While that lower figure is roughly half the current U.S. annual formal nullity total, it remains over 100 times higher than the pre-APN numbers in America.

15 The *1994 Catholic Almanac*, 235, suggests that at least 6 million American Catholics have been divorced at least one time. Lawrence Wrenn estimated that, in the late 1970s, only one-half of one percent of all divorced Catholics in America were receiving annulments each year. *CLSA Commentary*, page 1010. V. Pospishil, "Response to Role of Law Award," *CLSA Proceedings* (1994) 270–273, at 272, suggests that over 160,000 Catholic couples (out of 1.1 million American divorces) split up each year, but that only 10% of those couples will ever file a nullity petition.

16 There is a third possibility: namely, that tens of thousands, perhaps hundreds of thousands, of American Catholics bring completely sufficient marriage skills to the altar, but then disregard natural and ecclesiastical law in divorcing each other and

(usually) remarrying outside of the Church, only to then turn around and seek an ecclesiastical annulment of their first marriage for reasons unrelated, and sometimes even antithetical, to the conjugal truth of their situation. Such a perverse exercise of the free will, on such a massive scale, is, as a matter of moral theology, possible. Whether this is a plausible explanation of the American annulment avalanche, I think, remains to be seen.

17 The statistics are basically correct. According to the *1994 Catholic Almanac*, 59,220,000 American Catholics make up 6.2 percent of the world's 949,578,000 Catholic population. In 1991, the U.S. accounted for 63,900 (79 percent) of the world's 80,700 annulments.

18 Mendonca, *Rotal Anthology*, pp. 590–698, takes 108 pages to list, by country of origin, all Rotal marriage cases from 1971 to 1988. Italy alone takes up 76 of those pages (compared to America's less than 7 pages), and a sampling of the Italian pages shows an affirmative rate of at least 50 percent.

19 Those pastors who do try to prevent a disaster-waiting-to-happen from getting married face numerous canonical obstacles to their efforts. See, for example, 1983 CIC 18, 213, 1058, and 1077. But see 1983 CIC 1071–1072.

Glossary of Major Terms

Advocate — an advisor, usually a degreed canon lawyer, who assists persons to present their cases in canonical actions, such as marriage nullity procedures.

Affirmative — a short-hand way of saying that an annulment was granted. Derived from the fact that the *dubia* was answered in the affirmative, that is, the nullity of the marriage was proved. Sometimes called a *constat* ("it is proven").

Annulment — a common term for what is more accurately called a declaration of matrimonial nullity, an official determination that what appeared to be a valid marriage was not one. Not a divorce.

Assessor — an advisor to a judge, not necessarily degreed in canon law but usually very knowledgeable in canon law, can be either a cleric or layperson

Auditor — a tribunal official, cleric or lay, often but not necessarily degreed in canon law, who assists in the investigation of a case. Auditors generally have the same authority as judges in gathering evidence in a case, but they do not make the final decision.

Canon — a specific, numbered, provision of canon law.

Canon law — the internal legal system of the Catholic Church, and the main body of ecclesiastical rules under which annulment cases are heard. Most of canon law is found in the Code of Canon Law.

Citation — Usually refers to the official notice given by the tribunal to the respondent that a marriage is being impugned by the petitioner. Sometimes refers also to the notice sent to witnesses that their cooperation is being requested.

Civil marriage — Marriage recognized by civil law, but not necessarily by canon law. The civil marriages of non-Catholics are usually presumed valid. The term is also used to describe an attempt at marriage made by Catholics without observing canonical form.

Code of Canon Law — the one volume book which contains the complete text of the 1,752 individual canons of Church law. Most recently issued for Roman Catholics in 1983.

Competence, Tribunal — canonical authority to hear a case; basically the same as jurisdiction.

Consent — the commitment of a person capable of marriage, given in accord with canonical form, to marriage as the Church understands and proclaims it.

Convalidation — popularly termed "having a marriage blessed in the Church," a convalidation is the renewal of consent necessary before a marriage can be recognized as valid if that marriage was entered into despite the presence of a nondispensed impediment, or with insufficient consent to marriage as the Church understands and proclaims it, or in violation of canonical form.

Declaration of Nullity — also, *declaration of matrimonial nullity* or *annulment.* The decision by a diocesan tribunal or other qualified canonical court that what appeared to be, from one or more points of view, a valid marriage, was not one.

Dubium, Dubia — an official Latin term that means a doubt about the validity of the impugned marriage.

Form — also, canonical form, the actual process by which a Catholic marries in the Church. Often does, but need not, take place during a wedding Mass.

Impediment — certain qualities, recognized under canon law, which, if present at the time of the wedding, render the person canonically incapable of entering valid marriage, despite good intentions and the observance of canonical form, if that was required.

Impugned — canonically questioned or put up for review; a marriage that is being officially investigated for possible nullity is being impugned.

Instance — a tribunal or ecclesiastical court; also, the trial heard in such courts. There are always two, and sometimes three, instances in affirmative annulment cases.

Libellus — literally a "little book," this is the paperwork submitted by a petitioner to start a marriage nullity case in the tribunal. Sometimes called a "petition."

Licit — done in accord with Church rules. Although most things in Church life which are done licitly are also done validly, a wedding can be licit, but still be found invalid.

Marriage — a permanent, exclusive relationship between a man and woman which is ordered toward the good of the spouses and the procreation and education of children. The marriages of two baptized (but not necessarily Catholic) persons are also sacramental.

Monitum — a Latin term meaning a suggestion, but not an order, by a bishop or by the tribunal that a person take certain steps before attempting another marriage in the Church, even though an annulment has already declared him or her free to marry in the Church.

Negative — a short-hand way of saying an annulment was not granted. Derived from the fact that the *dubia* was answered in the negative, that is, nullity was not proved. Sometimes called a *non constat* (it is not proven).

Null — something which, even despite appearances to the contrary, was of no force from its beginning.

Parties — the petitioner and the respondent in an annulment case, the former spouses of the marriage.

Petition — also *libellus* (little book), the documents submitted by the petitioner in which the petitioner's request for an annulment is presented.

Petitioner — the person who files for an annulment. The petitioner can be either the husband or the wife. In some cases, the Promoter of Justice can file an annulment case.

Prohibition — an order sometimes placed on either or both parties to a null marriage which, despite the granting of the annulment, forbids remarriage in the Church until certain conditions are satisfied. Sometimes called *vetitum* (prohibition).

Radical Sanation — much like a convalidation, but not requiring a renewal of consent. Not used often.

Renunciation — withdrawing a nullity petition before it is adjudicated.

Rescript — an official, written answer, usually in response to a request for something; a dispensation.

Respondent — the other spouse in an annulment case, the one who is asked to respond to the filing of an annulment.

Tribunal — a panel of one or three canonical judges, appointed to office by the diocesan bishop, which decides whether canonical cases like annulments have been filed and proven in accord with canon law.

Valid — canonically binding and requiring respect by the Church. Not necessarily licit, but juridically effective in its goal.

Vetitum — see "Prohibition."

INDEX

Pauline privilege, 28, 50, 80, 84

Pregnancy, 46, 47, 94, 100

Pre-nuptial agreements, 96

Presumed death cases, 31

Prohibition. See *Vetitum*

Promoter of justice, 11, 16, 40, 93

Radical sanation, 28

Religious life, 33

Renunciation 23, 25

Roman authorities, 7, 8, 21, 22, 50, 63, 86

Separation, 48, 80, 82, 95

Vetitum, 46, 58, 77, 78

INDEX OF CANONS CITED

Canon #	Question #
1057 § 2	93
1058	77, 85
1060	32, 64, 72, 85, 100
1061 § 3	76
1062 § 2	45
1063, n.2	45
1065 § 1	53
1065 § 2	53, 95
1066	89, 96
1071 § 1, n.3	58
1075	77
1075, n.1	37
1076	77
1077	43, 58, 77
1077 § 1	77
1083	46, 49
1084	49, 51
1085	49, 87, 93
1085 § 1	28, 77
1085 § 2	28
1086	49
1086 § 1	50
1087	49
1088	49
1089	49
1090	49
1091	49
1092	49
1093	49
1094	49

Canon #	Question #
1158	30, 95
1159	30, 95
1160	30, 50
1161	28
1162	28
1163	28
1164	28
1165	28
1313 § 2	83
1388	71
1391	85
1400	41
1401	41
1401, n.1	26
1407 § 3	20
1415	20, 81
1417 § 1	22, 63
1417 § 2	63
1419 § 1	13
1420	13
1421	11, 13
1421 § 2	12
1421 § 3	12
1424	11
1425 § 3	11
1425 § 4	13
1426 § 1	12
1428 § 1	11
1429	12
1430	16, 81
1432	15

Canon #	*Question #*
1508 § 1	59
1509	59
1510	54, 60
1511	57, 64
1512, n.2	20, 23, 63, 81
1513	51, 62
1514	62
1515	62
1516	62
1520	25
1524	81, 25
1526	46, 64, 72, 85
1528	24
1530	24, 72
1531 § 1	60
1531 § 2	25, 54, 62
1535	72
1536	72
1536 § 2	72
1547	66, 70, 73
1548 § 2, n.1	71
1548 § 2, n.2	73
1550	69
1550 § 2, n.2	71
1553	62, 69
1555	69
1557	73
1558 § 1	67
1560	67
1561	67
1562	67

Canon #	Question #
1570	76
1571	6
1572	72
1573	72
1574	14, 49, 66
1575	66, 70
1580	6, 70
1581	70
1592	25, 54. 60, 64
1593	25, 64
1594	25
1595	25
1598	56, 70, 73
1598 § 1	55
1601	15
1602	15
1603	15
1604 § 1	55
1606	7, 24
1608	85
1608 § 4	64, 72
1610 § 2	12
1620	20, 54
1620, n.7	62, 65
1628	15, 22, 58, 63, 81
1643	57, 81
1649	5, 6
1671	26, 41
1672	58
1673	20, 61

About the Author

D r. Edward N. Peters received his civil law degree from the University of Missouri at Columbia and his doctoral degree in canon law from the Catholic University of America. He has held a number of teaching and administrative posts, including Director of the Office for Canonical Affairs for the Diocese of San Diego as well as Defender of the Bond and collegiate judge on diocesan and archdiocesan appellate tribunals. He currently is professor of canon law for the Institute for Pastoral Theology in Ypsilanti, Michigan. A frequent guest on Catholic media apostolates, Dr. Peters' articles and reviews have appeared in a wide variety of Catholic and secular publications. He maintains a canon law website, www.canonlaw.info, and serves as a consultant to many ecclesiastical institutions and persons. He and his wife, Angela, are raising six children.